Shakespear's Dramatic Techniques

Shakespear's Dramatic Techniques

Professor (Dr.) Samrendra Sharma

IJMRA PUBLICATIONS

Shakespear's Dramatic Techniques

Edition 2024

ISBN 978-93-87176-53-9

Published by:
IJMRA PUBLICATIONS
USA Office:
5913 Warren Ridge Dr, Bakersfield
California, USA-93313
India Office:
7 Sec 17, HUDA, Jagadhri-135003, India

Acknowledgements

Writing a book is always a matter of some inspiration at one point of time. My association with Sh Vinod Khanna actor-turned politician remained full of interactions and discussions which were more literary than anything else. His narration of how technicians in the making of a movie play very vital roles to express the ideas in a better manner was the point where I started revisiting Shakespeare whom I had read and appreciated during my post graduate days and taught for years together. So first of all I thank Sh.Vinod Khanna for making me understand the dramatic techniques in a better manner and hence publication of this book.

My thanks go to the librarians of BUC college Batala and SMDRSD college Pathankot who provided me with all the materials (books, journals etc) whenever I needed.

I will be failing in my primary duties if I don't acknowledge the contribution of my teachers who taught me Shakespeare. They Dr Paul Love and Prof Rita Mann of Baring Union Christian College Batala. Their expertise in correlating the dramatic techniques with the contents of the plays opened my faculties to understand the things in a better manner. My brother Dr Dinesh Principal AB college Pathankot has always been very helpful in clearing the cobwebs surrounding the topic if there were any.Last but not the least I thank my publishers. To bring out the book so that the ideas I had in my mind could be transmitted to everyone.

Thanks to Almighty God for everything.

Samrendra Sharma

Principal SMDRSD College Pathankot

Preface

William Shakespeare uses dramatic techniques – strategies that help a playwright present his story on stage – in his comedies and tragedies to capture the audience's attention. His characters often speak directly to the audience, and he uses recurring symbols to draw viewers into the play. Shakespeare relies on dramatic irony to add suspense, such as revealing hidden truths and incorporating twists into the plot that the characters seemingly know nothing about.

Shakespeare uses monologues and soliloquies – individual speeches by characters in the play – to reveal the character's feelings and provide background information necessary to the plot, climax or resolution. Monologues and soliloquies give scenes an emotional, personalized appeal.

Visual cues, such as recurring images and symbols, foreshadow events and help viewers connect ideas and themes throughout the story. This dramatic technique helps the audience see, not just hear, important details about the play. For example, Shakespeare repeatedly contrasts light and darkness in "Romeo and Juliet," foreshadowing the eventual demise of forbidden love. In "Othello," Shakespeare uses a handkerchief to symbolize love and purity. When Desdemona loses the handkerchief, it represents her unfaithfulness to Othello.

An aside – a moment when a character breaks from the scene and speaks to the audience without other characters hearing or reacting – happens only in performances. It's difficult to use asides in written works, because there's no easy way to demonstrate these frozen moments that allow characters to talk directly to readers.

Shakespeare's plays often feature situations in which the audience or another character has a better understanding of events than a central character does. This is dramatic irony, and he uses it to incorporate humor, confusion and conflict into his plays. As a result, characters often react carelessly or foolishly because they lack knowledge, insight and self-awareness. So these are some of the dramatic techniques which Shakespeare often used in his plays.

Contents

INTRODUCTION

Shakespeare's' Dramatic Techniques

Many people think of William Shakespeare as the greatest creative writer in the history of English literature (though there are a number of other candidates), and there is good reason for that. His influence on subsequent writers - not only English writers - is far-reaching and profound.

Through all the periods of literature, when some new literary technique or other seems to have been developed by a writer, on closer examination one finds something interesting: that Shakespeare has used that technique somewhere in his texts. For example, what is called 'stream of consciousness,' a technique very effectively used by James Joyce in Ulysses, was used by Shakespeare, notably in King Lear. Or, we call Harold Pinter's style of employing cryptic dialogue filled with spaces and silences 'Pinteresque,' as though that were a technique invented by Pinter. It has been copied by many writers. Shakespeare used that style frequently. The breathless conversation between Macbeth and Lady Macbeth immediately after Macbeth has murdered Duncan is decidedly 'Pinteresque.' Look at the below piece of dialogue and see how Shakespeare creates fear, apprehension and the sense that the characters can hardly believe what they've done by the use of sharp, whispered, sometimes disconnected bursts of language punctuated with silences:

'I have done the deed. Didst thou not hear a noise?'

'I heard the owl scream and the crickets cry. Did not you speak?'

'When?'

'Now.'

'As I descended?'

'Ay.'

'Hark! Who lies in the second chamber?'

'Donalbain.'

'This is a sorry sight.'

'A foolish thought, to say a sorry sight.'

The dialogue is a literary device. The term 'literary device' refers to the structures writers use in their creative writing to communicate with their audiences. Presenting a story about people to a reader or an audience, making the characters seem like real people in real situations in real places, doing things that real people do – fighting, falling in love, dying – is a trick because they are not real people doing real things. The writer has the task of making the audience identify with the characters and events of the story and to do that he or she uses an array of devices to help him or her create the illusion of reality. The better the writer is at doing that and the greater the mastery the writer has of the range of literary devices the more effective the work will be. Shakespeare is that writer, right at the top of the scale.

Shakespeare used many literary devices (and also many poetic devices) – below are the most important ones, most central to his work.

1. Allusion

This is a reference to a person, place, event, usually without explicit identification. Allusions can be references to mythology, the bible, historical events, geography, legends, or other literary works. Authors often use allusion to establish a tone, create an implied association, contrast two objects or people, make an unusual juxtaposition of references, or bring the reader into a world of experience outside the limitations of the story itself. Biblical references are common in literary works of all periods. Shakespeare's plots are frequently based on legends and historical events, which are also merely referred to in other plays. Shakespeare was fond of alluding to mythology and one of his most effective uses of that is in Antony and Cleopatra where the earthly lovers are frequently described in terms of Roman gods. In that play the lovers transcend the limits of ordinary earthly romantic love, and the imagery reflects and illuminates that idea.

2. Dramatic Device

Dramatic devices were not invented by Shakespeare as a drama would not hold up without them: the plays of Shakespeare's predecessors and contemporaries used them, but one of the reasons that Shakespeare's plays are so gripping and suspenseful is that he was a master of the dramatic device. A dramatic device is anything that drives the action. In Shakespeare's plays they come one after another, each one following closely on the previous one. In Macbeth, for example, the witches plant the idea of becoming king in Macbeth's mind, which leads him to raise it with his wife, who encourages him to kill Duncan, which he does. There are two dramatic devices for a start. Duncan's arrival at Glamys is another. And then comes the murder of Duncan, an enormous dramatic device, which creates all kinds of movement. And so it goes on, one after another, each one the result of the previous one, hurling the action forward, until the last moment of the drama.

3. Dramatic Irony

Dramatic irony is a situation in which the reader knows something about present or future circumstances that the character does not know. For example, in Macbeth, when Duncan's murdered body is found Macbeth behaves as though he's angry with the supposed murderers but the audience knows that he is in fact the murderer. That's dramatic irony.

4. Soliloquy

A speech in which a character, who is usually alone on the stage, expresses his or her thoughts aloud. It is a very useful device, as it allows the writer to convey a character's most intimate thoughts and feelings directly to the audience. The convention is that the audience is allowed to hear the character's thoughts. He or she is not talking, but thinking. Shakespeare uses soliloquies liberally, and some of his finest pieces of writing are in this form, for example the 'To be or not to be' soliloquy in Hamlet.

5. Symbolism

Shakespeare's use of symbolism is one of his strongest, most distinguishing characteristic. It is the frequent use of words, places, characters, or objects that mean something beyond what they are on a literal level. If, for example, a writer uses the word 'blood' once its meaning will be confined to that instance in which it is used. But if the word is used repeatedly, as it is in plays like Macbeth and Romeo and Juliet it expresses some profound ideas. By using a word repeatedly in different contexts it expresses several interlocking themes. In Romeo and Juliet 'blood' refers to all the following and more themes: violence, youth, passion, family ties. In King Lear this technique is particularly well developed. One strand of imagery refers to wild animals with sharp teeth, talons and claws, reflecting the savage and cruel way the members of the younger generation treat their elders, and giving clear images of the pain suffered by Lear and Gloucester.

6. Monologue

Shakespeare's plays are strewn with monologues - a long, uninterrupted speech that is spoken in the presence of other characters. Unlike a soliloquy a monologue is heard by other characters.

STYLE

Shakespeare's first plays were written in the conventional style of the day. He wrote them in a stylised language that does not always spring naturally from the needs of the characters or the drama. The poetry depends on extended, sometimes elaborate metaphors and conceits, and the language is often rhetorical—written for actors to declaim rather than speak. The grand speeches in Titus Andronicus, in the view of some critics, often hold up the action, for example; and the verse in The Two Gentlemen of Verona has been described as stilte.

However, Shakespeare soon began to adapt the traditional styles to his own purposes. The opening soliloquy of Richard III has its roots in the self-declaration of Vice in medieval drama. At the same time, Richard's vivid self-awareness looks forward to the soliloquies of Shakespeare's mature plays. No single play marks a change from the traditional to the freer style. Shakespeare combined the two throughout his career, with Romeo and Juliet perhaps the best example of the mixing of the styles. By the time of Romeo and Juliet, Richard II, and A Midsummer Night's Dream in the mid-1590s, Shakespeare had begun to write a more natural poetry. He increasingly tuned his metaphors and images to the needs of the drama itself.

Shakespeare's standard poetic form was blank verse, composed in iambic pentameter. In practice, this meant that his verse was usually unrhymed and consisted of ten syllables to a line, spoken with a stress on every second syllable. The blank verse of his early plays is quite different from that of his later ones. It is often beautiful, but its sentences tend to start, pause, and finish at the end of lines, with the risk of monotony.Once Shakespeare mastered traditional blank verse, he began to interrupt and vary its flow. This technique releases the new power and flexibility of the poetry in plays such as Julius Caesar and Hamlet. Shakespeare uses it, for example, to convey the turmoil in Hamlet's mind

Sir, in my heart there was a kind of fighting
That would not let me sleep. Methought I lay
Worse than the mutines in the bilboes. Rashly—
And prais'd be rashness for it—let us know
Our indiscretion sometimes serves us well ...

— *Hamlet, Act 5, Scene 2, 4–8*

After Hamlet, Shakespeare varied his poetic style further, particularly in the more emotional passages of the late tragedies. The literary critic A. C. Bradley described this style as "more concentrated, rapid, varied, and, in construction, less regular, not seldom twisted or elliptical".In the last phase of his career, Shakespeare adopted many techniques to achieve these effects. These included run-on lines, irregular pauses and stops, and extreme variations in sentence structure and length. In Macbeth, for example, the language darts from one unrelated metaphor or simile to another: "was the hope drunk/ Wherein you dressed yourself?" (1.7.35–38); "... pity, like a naked new-born babe/ Striding the blast, or heaven's cherubim, hors'd/ Upon the sightless couriers of the air ..." (1.7.21–25). The listener is challenged to complete the sense. The late romances, with their shifts in time and surprising turns of plot, inspired a last poetic style in which long and short sentences are set against one another, clauses are piled up, subject and object are reversed, and words are omitted, creating an effect of spontaneity.

Shakespeare combined poetic genius with a practical sense of the theatre. Like all playwrights of the time, he dramatised stories from sources such as Plutarch and Holinshed. He reshaped each plot to create several centres of interest and to show as many sides of a narrative to the audience as possible. This strength of design ensures that a Shakespeare play can survive translation, cutting and wide interpretation without loss to its core drama. As Shakespeare's mastery grew, he gave his characters clearer and more varied motivations and distinctive patterns of speech. He preserved aspects of his earlier style in the later plays, however. In Shakespeare's late romances, he deliberately returned to a more artificial style, which emphasised the illusion of theatre.

INFLUENCE

Shakespeare's work has made a lasting impression on later theatre and literature. In particular, he expanded the dramatic potential of characterisation, plot, language, and genre. Until Romeo and Juliet, for example, romance had not been viewed as a worthy topic for tragedy. Soliloquies had been used mainly to convey information about characters or events, but Shakespeare used them to explore characters' minds. His work heavily influenced later poetry. The Romantic poets attempted to revive Shakespearean verse drama, though with little success. Critic George Steiner described all English verse dramas from Coleridge to Tennyson as "feeble variations on Shakespearean themes."

Shakespeare influenced novelists such as Thomas Hardy, William Faulkner, and Charles Dickens. The American novelist Herman Melville's soliloquies owe much to Shakespeare; his Captain Ahab in Moby-Dick is a classic tragic hero, inspired by King Lear. Scholars have identified 20,000 pieces of music linked to Shakespeare's works. These include three operas by Giuseppe Verdi, Macbeth, Otello and Falstaff, whose critical standing compares with that of the source plays. Shakespeare has also inspired many painters, including the Romantics and the Pre-Raphaelites. The Swiss Romantic artist Henry Fuseli, a friend of William Blake, even translated Macbeth into German. The psychoanalyst Sigmund Freud drew on Shakespearean psychology, in particular, that of Hamlet, for his theories of human nature. In Shakespeare's day, English grammar, spelling, and pronunciation were less standardised than they are now, and his use of language helped shape modern English. Samuel Johnson quoted him more often than any other author in his A Dictionary of the English Language, the first serious work of its type. Expressions such as "with bated breath" (Merchant of Venice) and "a foregone conclusion" (Othello) have found their way into everyday English speech. Shakespeare's influence extends far beyond his native England and the English language. His reception in Germany was particularly significant; as early as the 18th century Shakespeare was widely translated and popularised in Germany, and gradually became a "classic of the German Weimar era;" Christoph Martin Wieland was the first to produce complete translations of Shakespeare's plays in any language.

CRITICAL REPUTATION

Shakespeare was not revered in his lifetime, but he received a large amount of praise. In 1598, the cleric and author Francis Meres singled him out from a group of English writers as "the most excellent" in both comedy and tragedy.The authors of the *Parnassus* plays at St John's College, Cambridge, numbered him with Chaucer, Gower, and Spenser. In the First Folio, Ben Jonson called Shakespeare the "Soul of the age, the applause, delight, the wonder of our stage", although he had remarked elsewhere that "Shakespeare wanted art".

Between the Restoration of the monarchy in 1660 and the end of the 17th century, classical ideas were in vogue. As a result, critics of the time mostly rated Shakespeare below John Fletcher and Ben Jonson. Thomas Rymer, for example, condemned Shakespeare for mixing the comic with the tragic. Nevertheless, poet and critic John Dryden rated Shakespeare highly, saying of Jonson, "I admire him, but I love Shakespeare". For several decades, Rymer's view held sway; but during the 18th century, critics began to respond to Shakespeare on his own terms and acclaim what they termed his natural genius. A series of scholarly editions of his work, notably those of Samuel Johnson in 1765 and Edmond Malone in 1790, added to his growing reputation. By 1800, he was firmly enshrined as the national poet. In the 18th and 19th centuries, his reputation also spread abroad. Among those who championed him were the writers Voltaire, Goethe, Stendhal, and Victor Hugo.

A recently garlanded statue of William Shakespeare in Lincoln Park, Chicago, typical of many created in the 19th and early 20th century

During the Romantic era, Shakespeare was praised by the poet and literary philosopher Samuel Taylor Coleridge, and the critic August Wilhelm Schlegel translated his plays in the spirit of German Romanticism. In the 19th century, critical admiration for Shakespeare's genius often bordered on adulation. "This King Shakespeare," the essayist Thomas Carlyle wrote in 1840, "does not he shine, in crowned sovereignty, over us all, as the noblest, gentlest, yet strongest of rallying signs; indestructible". The Victorians produced his plays as lavish spectacles on a grand scale. The playwright and critic George Bernard Shaw mocked the cult of Shakespeare worship as "bardolatry", claiming that the new naturalism of Ibsen's plays had made Shakespeare obsolete.

The modernist revolution in the arts during the early 20th century, far from discarding Shakespeare, eagerly enlisted his work in the service of the avant-garde. The Expressionists in Germany and the Futurists in Moscow mounted productions of his plays. Marxist playwright and director Bertolt Brecht devised an epic theatre under the influence of Shakespeare. The poet and critic T.S. Eliot argued against Shaw that Shakespeare's "primitiveness" in fact made him truly modern. Eliot, along with G. Wilson Knight and the school of New Criticism, led a movement towards a closer reading of Shakespeare's imagery. In the 1950s, a wave of new critical approaches replaced modernism and paved the way for "post-modern" studies of Shakespeare. By the 1980s, Shakespeare studies were open to movements such as structuralism, feminism, New Historicism, African-American studies, and queer studies. Comparing Shakespeare's accomplishments to those of leading figures in philosophy and theology, Harold Bloom wrote: "Shakespeare was larger than Plato and than St. Augustine. He *encloses* us because we *see* with his fundamental perceptions.

WORKS

Shakespeare's works include the 36 plays printed in the First Folio of 1623, listed according to their folio classification as comedies, histories, and tragedies. Two plays not included in the First Folio, The Two Noble Kinsmen and Pericles, Prince of

Tyre, are now accepted as part of the canon, with today's scholars agreeing that Shakespeare made major contributions to the writing of both. No Shakespearean poems were included in the First Folio.

In the late 19th century, Edward Dowden classified four of the late comedies as romances, and though many scholars prefer to call them tragicomedies, Dowden's term is often used. In 1896, Frederick S. Boas coined the term "problem plays" to describe four plays: All's Well That Ends Well, Measure for Measure, Troilus and Cressida, and Hamlet. "Dramas as singular in theme and temper cannot be strictly called comedies or tragedies", he wrote. "We may, therefore, borrow a convenient phrase from the theatre of today and class them together as Shakespeare's problem plays." The term, much debated and sometimes applied to other plays, remains in use, though Hamlet is definitively classed as a tragedy

CHAPTER I

ALLUSIONS IN SHAKESPEARE

TRAGEDY OF HAMLET, PRINCE OF DENMARK (1603)

When the reader of Shakespeare's works compares the language of *Hamlet* to that of such tragedies as *Macbeth* or *Titus Andronicus,* he realizes how few classical allusions there are in this, arguably Shakespeare's greatest play. However, though relatively few, the classical allusions in *Hamlet* are indeed telling. In *Titus Andronicus,* in contrast, Shakespeare through his characters is continually referring to a single classical work, *The Metamorphoses,* and in particular the Ovidian tale of Tereus, Procne and Philomela, an epyllion that presents the same grisly theme embodied in Shakespeare's play: in seeking a personal justice outside the Law the revenger may become as depraved as the evil he has determined to destroy. But in the classical allusions of *The Tragedy of Hamlet, Prince of Denmark* the bard does not merely suggest literary analogues or thematic parallels. Rather, these devices further our understanding of the way in which Hamlet views others in the play and himself since the single greatest source of classical allusions in the play is the eponymous character himself.

Since the play's backdrop is Christian Denmark in the early Renaissance (rather than pagan Rome in its decline, as it is in *Titus Andronicus,* for example), it is natural that most of the characters in *Hamlet* do not frame their thoughts in terms of Graeco-Roman culture. In terms of speech, what is appropriate for the characters in the Roman plays [1] is not suitable for Claudius' court. However, because Prince Hamlet has just returned from

Wittenberg University his references to classical myth and history are quite natural. By analyzing these references we may discover his personal definitions of Old Hamlet, Claudius, Gertrude, Rosencrantz, Guildenstern, of the golden world under his father's rule, of the fallen world under his uncle's rule, and ultimately of himself.

In pondering Claudius' utter substitution of himself in the bed as well as on the throne of Old Hamlet, the moody Prince in Act One, Scene Two, line 140, compares his deceased father to Hyperion, the Greek sun god, and the usurping Claudius to a satyr, a Greek mythic amalgam of man and goat. The comparison is apt when one recalls that the satyr was held to be the very epitome of animal lust and carnal passion. In Act Three, Scene Four, Hamlet develops the other aspect of the metaphor, once again in comparing his father to his uncle. "Look here upon this picture," he urges his mother, Queen Gertrude:

> and on this,
> The counterfeit presentment of two brothers,
> See what a grace was seated on this brow:
> Hyperion's curls, the front of Jove himself,
> An eye like Mars, to threaten and command,
> A station like the herald Mercury
> New lighted on a heaven-kissing hill . . . .[2]

In no uncertain terms, Hamlet holds his father up to his mother as a divinity who combines the best aspects of the chief Graeco-Roman deities: Old Hamlet was (if we follow the logic or mental processes of these allusions) as enlightened and dazzlingly attractive as the sun god, as wise and majestic as the king of the gods, as valorous and able to take charge of military affairs as the war god, and as dignified and youthful in his bearing as the messenger of the gods. Hamlet, in employing such similes, however, reveals that he has not accepted his father's mortality; in short, by comparing his father to gods, Hamlet shows that he cannot accept the fact that his father has died. Nor does the son acknowledge the many "imperfections" (I. V. 84) in character that the Ghost confesses he possessed in life. Nevertheless, the image of his father "Unhouseled, disappointed, unaneled, / No reckoning made" (I. V. 82-3) obsesses him, as is evident in the scene in Gertrude's closet, in which for Hamlet the Ghost serves as the reviver of memory.

She, lacking so powerful a memory of her first husband and (associated with this deficiency) so scrupulous a moral sense, seems to have completely replaced Old Hamlet's image for that of Claudius, not only in the concrete image worn on her breast, but also in her heart. In his initial soliloquy, Hamlet imagines her at his father's funeral "Like Niobe, all tears" (I. ii. 151). Again, Hamlet expresses himself in a classical commonplace: Niobe, who witnessed the destruction her whole family as *nemesis* for her own arrogance towards the mother of Apollo and Artemis, epitomizes grief as Hyperion does majestic (male) beauty. But this allusion, unlike that to Hyperion, involves a human and flawed figure in an Ovidian tale. The image suggests more than grief, for Niobe was in effect responsible for the deaths of those whom she mourned. And at this point in the play, before consulting with the Ghost in Act One, Scene Four, Hamlet suspects both Claudius and Gertrude of involvement in his father's untimely demise. The metaphor, therefore, reveals something of this suspicion of his mother and stepfather since they married so quickly after his father's death.

So far Hamlet's classical allusions have defined how he sees others: the King is a lustful beast, his father a dazzling god, his mother a foolish sinner. The images by which he defines himself are of far greater significance. For Hamlet, his father's usurping brother is no more like his father "Than I to Hercules" (I. ii. 153). Taken at face value, the remark indicates the speaker's self-deprecation and sense of unworthiness; Hamlet's image suggests that he sees himself as unheroic and incapable of noble action. But several other references to this Graeco-Roman demi-god provide further insight into Hamlet's psychology.

Hamlet, thrusting aside his friend Horatio to follow the Ghost, proclaims that "each petty artere in this body [has been rendered by the role which Fate has thrust upon him] As hardy as the Nemean lion's nerve" (I. iv. 82-3). The allusion is to the mythical beast slain by Hercules in the first of the twelve labours, necessary to expiate his murdering his wife in a fit of insanity sent by his jealous step-mother. Hercules was justly proud of his vanquishing a beast whose hide was so tough no weapon could pierce it and proclaimed this feat ever afterward by wearing the lion's hide instead of armour. For Hamlet, following the Ghost, which might well be a visitation of the Devil, calls for the same heroic determination as the classical demi-god required to accomplish that labour. However, Hamlet, as he admitted earlier, is not naturally suited to such a role—rather, his "fate cries out" (I. iv. 81) from beyond the grave and he is morally obligated to follow.

The Ghost, fresh from the classical underworld ("Lethe wharf," I. v. 33), speaks in very general Judeo-Christian terms such as "matin" (I. v. 94) rather than in classical images, but for the significant simile, when he mentions "Lethe wharf"(I, v, 33). Already, he suggests, he has begun the process of weaning himself away from the earth by drinking the waters of forgetfulness of the Underworld river. Yet, even so, he has returned to goad the memory of his son into revenge, a motive as un-Christian as his allusion. It is from those tranquilizing streams, moreover, Hamlet must be prohibited if he is to rouse himself to undertake the mission with which the Ghost now charges him. Specifically, the Ghost charges Hamlet, his potential avenger, "Remember me" (I. v. 96).

After Hamlet's confrontation with the Ghost, the classical allusions, particularly those to the demi-god Hercules, are somewhat more complex. The first example occurs in a discussion of the arrival of the actors at Elsinore. According to Rosencrantz, "an eyrie of children" (II, ii, 346), those companies of child-actors that in Shakespeare's London were providing fierce (and unfair) competition for the established adult acting companies, have apparently stolen the public's imagination. So effective have these child-actors been that they have cut into the business of the Globe itself, presented by its sign: "Hercules and his load" (II. ii. 369). Undeserving of commercial success, these children, like

Claudius, have borne all before them because the theatre-going public has forgotten the fine work of the professional acting companies of the metropolis. The whole image is one of substitution: in myth, Hercules held up the world while the Titan Atlas, who usually performed that task, carried off the apples from the Garden of the Hesperides for the hero. Similarly, children have replaced adults on the stage in the metropolis (not Copenhagen, but London), and a usurper has seized the throne of Denmark. Finally, a moody, introspective scholar has been called upon to act the part of a man of action and correct the political inversion.

Despite his apparently friendly discussion with Rosencrantz and Guildenstern, Hamlet distrusts them. As he later confides to Gertrude, "my two schoolfellows . . . I will trust as I will adders fanged" (III. iv. 204). Superficially, he likens them to poisonous-snakes, poison being a dominant motif in the play. But the recurring references to Hercules may fit here, too. In Book IX of Ovid's *Metamorphoses* Hercules brags of strangling the pair of serpents that the jealous goddess Juno had sent to destroy him while he was yet an infant sleeping in his crib. Like those mythic beasts, Rosencrantz and Guildenstern are to be the tools of a malignant higher power (in this case, Claudius) in the destruction of the hero. Later, almost as unexpectedly as the infant Hercules' eliminating the snakes comes the revelation that Hamlet has destroyed the King's agents with their own commission!

All the allusions discussed so far have been spontaneous in their utterance, being employed chiefly in metaphors and similes. However. Hamlet's allusion to Aeneas's after-dinner narrative for Dido's court in Virgil's *Aeneid* is conscious and intentional. Hamlet recalls "Priam's slaughter" (II. ii. 454) by Pyrrhus in revenge for the ignominious death of his father, Achilles, effected by the poisoned arrow of Paris. Although one would expect Hamlet to identify himself with the avenging son, the quality of language in the set speech tends to indicate his sympathy with the old Trojan King. This confusion lies partly in Hamlet's repugnance at the thought of actually having to take revenge himself and partly in his identification of the victim with his father and the killer with Claudius. Hence, as Pyrrhus advances towards the subject of his revenge, he resembles "th' Hyrcanian beast" (II. ii. 456) rather than the invincible warrior of Book Two in *The Aeneid.* Hence, "Pyrrhus' bleeding sword" (II. ii. 498) falls with the force of a hammer wielded by a Cyclops, a one-eyed, savage giant who labours for the smith of the gods, Vulcan or Haephestus. In fact, Hamlet uses "Vulcan's Stithy" (III. ii. 84) as a metaphor of foulness for his mind if it has only imagined that the Ghost has designated Claudius as Old Hamlet's killer. Pyrrhus as revenger, then, is described by Hamlet as bestial and by the Player as freakish and quasi-human. Such is the type of man who pursues what Bacon termed "a kind of wild justice." [3]

Freudian critics undoubtedly have made much of Hamlet's insistence that the Player hurry the speech to "come to Hecuba" (II. ii. 508), for his interest in the grieving Trojan Queen may reflect his obsession with his mother, the "Mobbled [muffled or disguised] queen" (II. ii. 510). However, unlike Gertrude, Queen of Denmark, Hecuba, Queen of Troy, was witness to her husband's death:

> When She saw Pyrrhus make malicious sport
> In mincing with his sword her husband's limbs,
> The instant burst of clamor that she made
> (Unless things mortal move them not at all)
> Would have much milch the burning eyes of heaven
> And passion in the gods. (II. ii. 520-525)

These words are not Hamlet's, of course, but the Lead Player's -however, they have, as it were, been placed in the Player's mouth by the Prince. As with the reference to Niobe earlier, Hamlet is utilizing a classical allusion for contrast: Niobe's grief, like Hecuba's, was paralyzing in its force, not so easily forgotten as Gertrude's apparently was. In Virgil's *Aeneid*, Hecuba is the very picture of grief, but in Ovid's *Metamorphoses* she signifies revenge, scratching out the eyes of her son's killer with her bare hands. Unlike Gertrude, Hecuba, after her husband's death, becomes "a queen of sorrows/Now a poor queen in chains, less than a slave." [4] While Gertrude has no tears to shed for Old Hamlet, Hecuba's "tears drowned in the desert of her grief" (p. 366). The player could counterfeit a passion when describing Hecuba's plight, but Hamlet cannot pity his mother because he is so choked with self-pity. With his mother's example before him, Hamlet cannot believe that a woman is capable of grief so passionate as his: he equates the character of Hecuba with a literary figment or construct, a "nothing" (II. ii. 562), for he cannot credit that woman is other than shallow and fickle.

The literary ornateness of the Player King's opening speech in "The Murder of Gonzago" (i. e., "The Mousetrap") seems sterile beside the passionate outbursts of Hamlet's soliloquy which contemplates Hecuba. In the play-within-the-play, the classical allusions are tedious periphrases: "Phoebus cart" signifies the annual revolution of the sun; "Neptune's salt wash" the ocean; and "Tellus'orbed ground" the earth. These elements the Player King calls upon as witnesses to the thirty years they have transpired since Hymen, the god of marriage, united him to the queen (the age of Hamlet, 29, points to the marriage of Gertrude and Hamlet Sr. as having lasted about 30 years).

Unfortunately, these conscious classical allusions have little of the deeper significance of those which leap unbidden to Hamlet's lips as fit metaphors for his passions. Later in that scene, for instance, when all have suddenly departed after Claudius' abrupt exit, Hamlet refers to Horatio as "Damon dear" and of his deceased father as "Jove himself" (III. ii. 285-7). The former allusion compares Hamlet's closest friend to the Syracusan Pythagorean who pledged his life to the tyrant Dionysius so that his friend Phintias might arrange his affairs before the tyrant's death sentence should be carried out on him. Although Damon was a classical commonplace for self-sacrificing friendship, Hamlet's allusion reveals that he believes Horatio would pledge his very life for Hamlet's own – in the end, Horatio does, in fact, express the desire to follow his friend into death. Thus, Hamlet consumes the poison that Horatio desires to take, asking him to live long enough to set the record straight. After "The Mousetrap" has unmasked Claudius, Hamlet realizes that only in Horatio does he have a friend whom he can trust implicitly, even with his life.

But what of the reference to Jove as Hamlet's father? Jove, king of gods and men, had may sons, all of whom were either gods or heroes (including Hercules). Now that Claudius' actions have confirmed the accusations of the Ghost, Hamlet realizes that he must prove himself his father's son and rise to the heroic role Fate has thrust upon him.

The final classical allusion to be considered comes not from Hamlet, but from his foil, Laertes (named after the former Argonaut and father of the cunning Odysseus in Homer's *Odyssey*). His calling upon "old Pelion" and "blue Olympus" (V. i. 253-254) to cover him and his sister, though he is alive and she dead, represents metaphorically his rebellion against the ordained nature of things and his determination to bury his sister with full Christian obsequies, despite the possibility that she may have committed suicide. He utters these words as a challenge from her grave, defying the gravediggers to "pile your dust upon the quick and dead" (V. i. 251) as the rebellious giants had piled Mount Pelion on top of Mount Olympus in their attempt to invade heaven, This, however, was a Babel-like hubris that met with the full fury of Jove's lightning. In contrast to this defiance of things as they must be, Hamlet in exile has learned that acceptance of one's fortunes is the answer to life's dilemmas: "The readiness is all" (V. ii. 224). No longer is his consciousness groping for expression in metaphor—as he sees clearly, he speaks clearly. Hence, Laertes begins as Hamlet had begun, giving vent to the anguish of his grief at the death of a loved one by means of classical allusion.

The use of classical allusions, then, is largely metaphorical. Hamlet utilizes classical references to define others and himself. In "The Mousetrap" classical allusions decorate the language, throwing an air of fantasy over the play-within-the-play. Finally Shakespeare has the impassioned Laertes speak in a Hamlet-like manner from Ophelia's grave to draw our attention to the similarity in his present situation and Hamlet's earlier. Ultimately, of course, these metaphors are limiting as well as psychologically revealing, for Hamlet, as he himself suggests, is not a Hercules – he is a hero of far greater yet subtler dimensions. Hamlet's noble and emotional utterances, in which his classical allusions are a significant feature, set him as far apart from the common herd of humanity as Hercules the legendary strongman and heroic demi-god of Graeco-Roman myth.

ALLUSIONS IN OTHELLO

Shakespeare's play *Othello* was written and first performed around 1603. It is the story of Othello, a Moor (or North African) who becomes an army general in the Italian city of Venice and marries Desdemona, the daughter of a senator. Othello's downfall comes when his evil underling Iago, angry after being passed over for promotion, tells Othello that Desdemona is having an affair with Cassio, Othello's lieutenant, who received the promotion over Iago. The jealousy of this perceived affair causes Othello to murder Desdemona.

Like all of Shakespeare's plays, *Othello* can be difficult for modern readers to understand. Much of this, of course, is due to the now outdated language that Shakespeare uses, since the play was written over 400 years ago. But another common cause of confusion for modern readers is Shakespeare's use of **allusion**.

An allusion simply means a reference to another work of literature or art. It is still used today in TV shows like *The Simpsons*, which frequently quotes lines or whole scenes from popular movies or other TV shows. When *The Simpsons* makes a reference to *The Godfather*, for example, the writers assume their audience, or at least most of them, will be familiar with *The Godfather* and understand the allusion.

Shakespeare did the same thing, making allusions that he assumed his audience would get. But he often referenced texts that are not as familiar to people today. Two of Shakespeare's favorite sources for allusions were the Bible and classical mythology.

Understanding Shakespeare's Biblical references is vital for the interpretation of many, if not all, of Shakespeare's plays. For *Othello*, it is especially important, not only because the interpretation of the play is contested among various approaches — feminist, homosexual, post-colonial, Marxist, Freudian, new historical, and others — but also and more importantly because, as I believe I can demonstrate, Shakespeare called attention to his Biblical references in a way that a contemporary audience would not have missed. I believe Shakespeare chose Biblical references that place the play in a specific framework, essential for appreciating its meaning.

Of course, for many scholars in our day, meaning is what the reader/viewer imposes on the text, not some unchangeable something that he finds already there.((There are, of course, problems with the idea of "unchangeable" meaning, but I do not have time to go into that in this essay. Suffice it to say that while certain aspects of a play's meaning necessarily change, there are other aspects that remain. "In many respects, then, meaning changes with the times because texts and their meanings are like events in several respects. The original writing and publication of a text is an event; my reading of that text is an event, or a series of events, caused by the text; and public interpretation and discussion of a text is another event caused by the original text." Peter Leithart, Deep Exegesis: The Mystery of Reading Scripture (Waco, Texas: Baylor University Press, 2009), p. 51. Leithart thoroughly explains the notion of meaning changing over time in the chapter titled "Texts Are Events.")) If we were to take such a view, there would be no real point in asking what Shakespeare might have been trying to do or how his original audience would have understood the play. We would be free to exploit the text for whatever cause we wished to endorse: Marxism, feminism, gay rights, or whatever. But if we think we ought to seek Shakespeare's meaning — to the degree that it is possible — we will have to consult his Biblical references, among other things. How so? Because the Biblical references in *Othello* were all added by Shakespeare to the original story he found in Cinthio. In addition, he significantly modified the story itself in order to fit the Biblically profound picture he drew.

Taking Biblical references into account also solves two basic and related problems that have plagued 20th century interpretation of the play. One, how can *Othello* be a great tragedy? Two, is Othello a noble Moor or just a fool? The two questions are obviously related. If, in the end, Othello is a mere fool duped by his "ancient," then the story of his fall can hardly be "great tragedy." But if *Othello* is great tragedy, we must be able to find a way to understand the Moor that does not reduce him to a rash dolt.

First, then, does *Othello* have the elements that go into making a great tragedy, tragedy with a capital "T"? Consider it in contrast with the Shakespeare's other great tragedies. Hamlet, Lear, and Macbeth all concern the murder of kings and the fall of kingdoms. As in the Biblical story of Adam, in each of these plays a single man's sin wreaks havoc in the "whole world." *Othello,* however, seems to lack that dimension. It is true that Venice and Cyprus are endangered by the Turks, but that threat is removed the first scene of Act II. When Othello finally falls into his tragic sin, there is no international crisis as a result, no kingdom in danger, no great loss of lives and property through war. Helen Gardner observed the following in 1967.

"Much of the criticism of *Othello* in this century has been marked by an uneasiness which was first voiced by Bradley. This was partly a consequence of his endeavour to discover and define the 'substance' of a Shakespearean Tragedy. Unable to deny that *Othello* was a masterpiece, and that if we are to distinguish certain of Shakespeare's tragedies as 'great tragedies' we must place *Othello* among them, he had in honesty to recognize that the vision of the world given by *Othello* did not conform to his conception of the vision of the world that the great tragedies present.... The reservation over the play's claim to supreme greatness he ascribed to the 'comparative confinement of the imaginative atmosphere.' '*Othello* has not . . . the power of dilating the imagination by vague suggestions of huge universal powers working in the world of individual fate and passion.' Compared with the other three 'great tragedies,' 'it is, in a sense, less "symbolic."' It leaves us with the impression that we are not 'in contact with the whole of Shakespeare;' and 'it is perhaps significant in this respect that the hero himself strikes us has having, probably, less of the poet's personality in him than many characters far inferior both as dramatic creations and as men.'((Helen Gardner, "'*Othello*:' A Retrospect, 1900-1967" in Shakespeare Survey: An Annual Survey of Shakespeare Study and Production, no. 21, edited by Kenneth Muir (Cambridge: University Press, 1968), p. 1.))"

Gardner goes on to say that "many have shared his [Bradley's] sense that the play lacks universal significance and a larger 'meaning' . . . ."((Ibid.)) The story seems to be limited to the domestic realm, with nothing transcendent, nothing universal suggested. The specific phrase "less symbolic" is particularly noteworthy. How, then, could it be tragedy with a capital "T"?((M. R. Ridley offers a partial answer to the problem when he suggests that because *Othello* has a clearly developed and dramatically powerful plot, it may be Shakespeare's best play – "in the narrow sense of 'theatre' probably much his best" – even though it is not his greatest work. He opines, "It has neither the variety nor the depth of Hamlet, none of the overwhelming power of Lear, none of that atmosphere which in Macbeth keeps us awfully hovering on the confines of a world outside that of our normal experience . . . But its grip upon the emotions of the audience is more relentless and sustained than that of the others. . . . from the moment of the landing in Cyprus the action moves fast, and the tension steadily mounts, with hardly an instant's relaxation, till the moment at which Othello kills himself . . ." He also comments that Aristotle's view that one of the features of great tragedy is "implication followed by explication" which is not found in the other three great tragedies, but is in *Othello*. Shakespeare, *Othello*, Arden edition, ed. M.R. Ridley (London: Meuthen, 1958), pp. xlv-xlvi.))

This entire way of viewing and reading *Othello*, this way of "problematizing" the play comes in part from ignoring Shakespeare's Elizabethan Christian worldview and the Scripture references that place the whole story within a specific symbolic context that make the play large with meaning. For Othello is an unusual but sophisticated version of the often-told story of the Fall — a favorite topic for plays from the Middle Ages onward. But modern audiences and even Shakespearean critics are not attuned to Biblical references or Biblical stories that resonate in the background of *Othello.*

"You don't know what you don't know. The popular adage has ramifications not only for realms of knowledge, but for ways of knowing. You don't know what you can't know because it is beyond your ways of knowing. In his influential book of a half-century ago, from which I have drawn my epigraph, Bernard Spivack presented a modulation of this idea: you don't see what you don't know. You can't perceive that which is beyond your modes of perception. In Spivack's account, a critical tradition of understanding the Shakespearean stage through the lens of naturalism had rendered certain elements of the plays invisible to the scholarly eye. In particular, critics were blind to the drama's affiliations with elements of supernaturalism carried forward from earlier religious drama, such as the Vice figure which, Spivack argues, underlies the character of Iago."((Kristen Poole, Supernatural Environments in Shakespeare's England: Spaces of Demonism, Divinity, and Drama (Cambridge: Cambridge University Press: 2011), pp. 58-59.))

Modern viewers of *Othello* do not see or hear some of what would have been loud-sounding and blatantly obvious to an Elizabethan viewer — the idea that the play is a story of the Fall of Man being perhaps highest on the list. The story of the fall is so far from the modern consciousness that we cannot see it, even if it is right in front of us in bold letters or sounded out in loudest tones. In Shakespeare's day, the story of Adam's fall was a paradigm story that was part of the everyday experiences of English people — in music, in Scripture reading, in pictures in churches, even in conversations about politics or history.

Perhaps some in our day may doubt that it would be possible for a "black" man((Othello's race is another controversial topic. Norman Sanders writes: "For the modern reader all of these indications of colour and race would almost certainly point to a

Negro; but for the seventeenth-century Londoner they could apply equally well to an Arab. Iago's derogatory comparison of Othello to a 'Barbary horse' (1.1.111-12) would not be taken by any member of the Blackfriars audience to be other than to an Arabian steed; and his scornful use of the term 'barbarian' (1.3.343) is exactly that used by Elizabeth's courtiers to refer to Abd el-Ouahed and his entourage. Even in the lie he tells Roderigo about Othello's demotion, it is Mauritania (i.e. the land of the Moors) he selects for the imaginary posting (4.2.217). More generally, it was the north African races that were popularly associated with the kinds of reactions that Othello manifests in the play . . ." Othello (The New Cambridge Shakespeare), p. 14. It seems to me that Sanders' conclusion here suggests strongly an Arabic Othello, but Sanders himself concludes that for people in our day, the role demands a Negroid Othello.)) to play the role of "everyman" in Elizabethan England. Although Othello's blackness marks him out as foreign, it does not necessarily suggest "inferior" in Shakespeare's day. Moreover, it was apparently the custom in Venice to hire foreigners.

"For Cinthio and his readers, as for the Venetians in the play, the spectacle of a foreign commander of Italian forces was nothing remarkable. Indeed, according to Contarino's study of the Republic, by long custom the city 'held it a better course to defend their dominions upon the Continent with foreign mercenary soldiers, than with their homeborn citizens;' and there was even a law that ensured that the general of the army was always foreign born."((Norman Sanders, *Othello*, p. 10.))

In addition, Othello's position at the head of the Venetian military would have been one of considerable prestige in a society in which the military retained a respect and social status quite different from our day.(("Whether he is facing Desdemona's irate father and her armed relatives, or answering the accusation of witchcraft before the full Senate, or dealing with a disciplinary problem on the watch, he demonstrates a capacity for swift decision, a monumental authority and a calm self-confidence that are characteristic of his kind. Unless we give the fullest emphasis to the ideal that lies behind these qualities and accept as valid Othello's view of himself as military man, the great farewell speech to his profession, with its spectacular sense of the glory and grandeur of war, becomes merely a mindless exercise in the glamorising of a peculiarly beastly job." Sanders, *Othello*, p. 22.)) Keeping in mind the military background, there was one man only in the Geneva Bible that viewers of the play could have associated with Othello: "Ebed-melech ye blacke More" (Jer. 38:7 ff.) The "blacke More" in the story of Jeremiah 38 is a heroic figure who bravely stands up for the persecuted Jeremiah and saves his life.((Altogether the expression "blacke More" appears in eight verses of the Geneva Bible (Jer 13:23; 38:7, 10, 12; 39:16; 46:9; Ezek 29:10; Dan 11:43), though only once in the Bishops Bible (2 Kgs 19:9).)) As his reward, God saves "Ebed-melech the blacke More" (Jer. 39:16) in the day of the Babylonian invasion. Only the Geneva translation of the Bible renders these verses as "blacke More," but since it was the most popular translation of Shakespeare's day, it is certainly possible for the association with Othello to be made. Even if Elizabethan viewers and readers of the play would not have directly associated the hero from Jeremiah, the fact remains that there is a "blacke More" hero in the Bible, as well as Solomon's black wife (Song 1:5)((In the Song of Solomon, the Geneva Bible has a note on the race of Solomon's bride, because she says she is "comely as the tentes of Kedar" which the Geneva Bible notes was in Arabia – another indication that in Shakespeare's day, Arabians were considered "black.")) and the possibility of Moses' black wife (Num. 12:1). While none of this means that it is not unusual to have a black Moor placed in the role of an "everyman" who falls into sin through the devil's temptation, it still provides background for our understanding and aids in appreciating Ludovico's summary statement of the story. We should read the word "Fallen" here with full theological meaning.

> Lodovico. O thou Othello, that wert once so good,
> Fallen in the practice of a damned slave
> What shall be said to thee? (5.2.287-89)

Thus, although Othello is "black" and foreign, he can be and is set forth as a symbol of "everyman."(("The debt to the old drama runs even deeper. Shakespeare found in it not only a model for individual characters but also a structural inspiration for some of his greatest scenes. Emrys Jones once identified Jesus's apprehension by torchlight in the Garden of Gethsemane—a set-piece in almost every mystery cycle—as the basis for the Venetian posse that hunts down Othello at the Sagittary Inn. On an even larger scale of influence, Iago's and Desdemona's competition for Othello's soul exposes the whole play as a tragic Mankind or Everyman in which the Vice triumphs." From the "Introduction" in Shakespeare and the Middle Ages, edited by Curtis Perry and John Watkins (Oxford: Oxford University Press, 2009), p. 4.)) This appears strikingly in the second scene of the first act when Shakespeare invents a scene that is not in Cinthio and includes a clear allusion to the Biblical story of the arrest of Christ in the Garden of Gesthemene. The specific language which alludes to the Biblical story is Othello's command: "Keep up your bright swords" (1.2.59).((Compare with Matthew 26:52: "Put up thy sword into his place." and John 18:11: "Put up thy sword into the sheath.")) Naseeb Shaheen offers the following illuminating comments.

"The setting closely parallels the Gospel accounts of Jesus' arrest. A band with torches and armed with swords comes by night to arrest Othello. The stage direction in the Quarto (1622) says: "Enters Brabantio, Roderigo, and others with lights and weapons." The stage direction in the Folio is: "Enter Brabantio, Roderigo, with Officers and Torches." The circumstances of Jesus arrest are much the same. Matthew 26.47; John 18.3."((Naseeb Shaheen, Biblical References in Shakespeare's Plays (Newark: University of Delaware Press, 1999), p. 583. The two passages Shaheen cites follow: "While he was still speaking, Judas came, one of the twelve, and with him a great crowd with swords and clubs, from the chief priests and the elders of the people. (Mat. 26:47); "So Judas, having procured a band of soldiers and some officers from the chief priests and the Pharisees, went there with lanterns and torches and weapons." (Joh. 18:3). My entire discussion here is indebted to Shaheen.))

As allusions go, this is clear enough in itself, but the fact that Shakespeare here added an incident that is not only not found in Cinthio's original story but even contradicts Cinthio's story line((Shaheen points out that in Cinthio there is no elopement and no attempt to arrest Othello. Desdemona and the Moor marry against the parents wishes, but without the complications in Shakespeare. They even live together happily for some time in Venice. Ibid.)) indicates clearly that this incident and its Biblical associations are important for what Shakespeare is doing in this play. All the more so, in that it is this scene in which we are finally introduced to the man that Iago had previously described at length in the most unflattering terms (1.1.9ff.). Othello's calm bearing and courage in the face of extreme danger, like Christ's in the Bible, draws attention to his dignity and offers dramatic refutation of Iago's slanders. That impression is only augmented by the trial scene that naturally follows the arrest. Though Othello is more loquacious at his trial than Christ was, his display of dignity, calm rationality, and courage is analogous.((Again, there is no trial scene in Cinthio's story. Though, of course, after an arrest, as is necessary, it is part of Shakespeare's Biblical allusion.))

In fact, since the arrest scene is associated with Othello's marriage to Desdemona, it suggests that Othello is a Christ-like husband to his bride – alluding to the well-known Biblical picture of Christ and His church. Though it may seem too much to regard the marriage of Othello and Desdemona as a picture of the marriage of Christ and the Church, in Elizabethan times the Anglican marriage rite included specific reference to the fact that all marriages signify "unto us the mystical union that is betwixt Christ and his Church."((From the 1559 Anglican Book of Common Prayer. Online: http://justus.anglican.org/resources/bcp/1559/Marriage_1559.htm.)) By making specific allusion to Christ at the very time that Othello and Desdemona are wed, Shakespeare ensures that we take note of the symbolism of marriage.

Two references to the Bible with regard to Desdemona confirm this allusive matrix. First, Brabantio, during Othello's trial, describes Desdemona as "A maiden never bold; Of spirit so still and quiet that her motion Blushed at herself" (1.3.94-96), alluding to 1 Peter 3:4-5. This suggests that she is an ideal Christian woman. Shortly after this, as Othello offers his defense against Brababtio's accusation, he describes Desdemona in language that recalls the Gospel story of Martha and Mary.

> . . . This to hear
> Would Desdemona seriously incline;
> But still the house affairs would draw her thence,
> Which ever as she could with haste dispatch
> She'd come again, and with a greedy ear
> Devour up my discourse; . . . (1.3.144-49)

In these two allusions to Scripture, then, Shakespeare suggests that Desdemona is a woman of exemplary character, as if she were a combination of Mary and Martha.((Both of the references here are noted by Shaheen, who suggested that Shakespeare combines Martha and Mary into one and points out that nothing like this is found in Cinthio's story. Shaheen, Op. Cit., p. 584.)) This also associates her with the story of Christ, reinforcing the parallel between Othello's marriage to her with Christ's to the church. Thus, to evoke Biblical associations with both Othello and Desdemona, Shakespeare modified Cinthio's story to add allusions that connect the Biblical story of Jesus with his Othello and to suggest the relationship between Christ and the church. This gives a transcendent dimension to the domestic realities of the play and makes the story of Othello a story of "Everyman." This qualifies as great tragedy because it is a retelling of the Fall of Man in the fall of Christ-like Othello.

Romeo and Juliet Allusion

A brief, indirect reference to a place, person, thing or idea that holds, historical, mythological or literary significance is called an allusion. The dramatist merely makes a passing reference to the allusion without going into detail. It is assumed that the audience or readers are aware of the philosophical or historical significance of the reference and can, therefore, understand its implication within the context of a play. In the vast majority of

Shakespearean tragedies, frequent allusions are made from Roman or Greek mythological figures and also from the Bible. Some of the most important allusions from "Romeo and Juliet" are given below:

Allusion in "Romeo and Juliet"

Example #1

"But all so soon as the all-cheering sun
Should in the farthest east begin to draw
The shady curtains from Aurora's bed,
Away from light steals home my heavy son"
(I.i. 137-140)

In these particular lines, Lord Montague refers to Aurora – the Roman goddess of dawn. Lord Montague expresses his concern for his son Romeo, stating that he has often seen Romeo crying at dawn. Moreover, Lord Montague maintains that Romeo's lack of enthusiasm for life is evident from the fact that something worries him and keeps him awake at nights. Hence, he often sleeps at dawn – the moment when the goddess Aurora awakes from her sleep and ascends the sky.

Example #2

"Well in that hit you miss. She'll not be hit
With Cupid's arrow. She hath Dian's wit,
And, in strong proof of chastity well armed,
From love's weak childish bow she lives uncharmed."
(I.i. 216-217)

The quote above is spoken by Romeo in relation to his first superficial love towards Rosaline and her refusal to respond to his love. Romeo makes a reference to Cupid, the Roman god of love, stating that Rosaline is so determined about not pursuing a relationship with Romeo that even Cupid cannot yield her otherwise. Moreover, Romeo makes another reference to Diana, the Roman goddess of hunting, women, and childbirth and states that similar to Diana, who vowed celibacy for life, Rosaline is fiercely inflexible and will never consent to marry Romeo.

Example #3

"You are a lover. Borrow Cupid's wings
And soar with them above a common bound."
(I. iv. 17-18)

In the lines above, Mercutio alludes to Cupid while offering advice to a love-sick Romeo. It is noteworthy that in classical mythology, Cupid's wings were often taken as a symbol of his unpredictable nature and were a manifestation of his ability to make people fall in and out of love very quickly. Using Cupid as a point of reference, Mercutio counsels Romeo that as a lover, Romeo should display more strength than an average man and exemplify Cupid's power in falling out of love with Rosaline.

Example #4

"O, then I see Queen Mab hath been with you.
She is the fairies' midwife, and she comes
In shape no bigger than an agate stone"
(I.iv. 58-60)

In the above quote, Mercutio makes a reference to Queen Mab, the queen of the fairies. He uses the allusion as a means to mock the huge significance Romeo places on his dreams. As a queen of the fairies, Queen Mab helped people in the fruition of their dreams. Mercutio tells Romeo that dreams are merely figments of one's thoughts, fears, and imagination. Hence, a grownup like Romeo getting unnerved by his dream is as absurd as an adult entertaining the Queen Mab fantasy.

Example #5

"When King Cophetua loved the beggar maid. -
He heareth not, he stirreth not, he moveth not."
(II.i. 17-18)

In this quote, Mercutio refers to the Medieval legend, King Cophetua who had never been in love until Cupid cast his spell on him, and the King instantly fell in love with a beggar. Mercutio further asserts that the King's newfound, unanticipated love for the beggar completely paralyzed him, rendering him incapable of thinking about anything else. Equating Romeo's predicament with King Cophetua, he alleges that like the King, Romeo cannot fathom thinking about anyone other than Rosaline.

Example #6

"Dost thou love me? I know thou wilt say "Ay,"
And I will take thy word. Yet, if thou swear'st,
Thou mayst prove false. At lovers' perjuries,
They say, Jove laughs."
(II.ii. 95-99)

In this famous quote from the acclaimed balcony scene, Juliet refers to Jove – the king of Gods in Roman mythology. It is noteworthy that Jove was notorious for his illicit affairs. One of Jove's duties was to ensure that people abide by their promises or pledges. However, after asking Romeo if he truly loves her, Juliet maintains that even if he were to lie about his loyalty, Jove would not be offended in the least since Jove pays no heed to unfaithful lovers retracting from their promises.

Example #7

"Else would I tear the cave where Echo lies
And make her airy tongue more hoarse than mine
With repetition of "My Romeo!"
(II.ii. 172-174)

After bidding farewell to Romeo in the balcony scene, Juliet eagerly asks Romeo to return soon. After that, Juliet makes a reference to Echo – the nymph featured in ancient Greek mythology. Echo fell in love with Narcissus. Unfortunately, he did not return her love in response to which Echo retreated to a cave and kept repeating the words of others. By alluding to Echo, Juliet is implying that if Romeo does not return, Juliet will find Echo and persuade her to repeat Romeo's name forever.

Example #8

"Tybalt, you ratcatcher, will you walk?"
(III.i. 76)

In the quote above, Mercutio, while conversing with Tybalt, Juliet's cousin, makes a reference to a character named Tybalt who is featured in a well-known Medieval tale "Reynard the Fox". The character Tybalt showcased in "Reynard the Fox" is quarrelsome and temperamental and is portrayed as a rat-catcher. Within the context of "Romeo and Juliet", Tybalt is depicted as an aggressive individual ever-ready to start a brawl. Hence, Mercutio equates Tybalt with his namesake character from the Medieval tale.

Example #9

"I am hurt.
A plague o' both houses! I am sped.
Is he gone and hath nothing?"
(III.i. 93-95)

After Mercutio is stabbed by Tybalt, he engages in an elaborate curse condemning the two families - Capulets, and Montagues for his demise. He prays and curses that they will be afflicted by the deadly plague. In this particular quote, plague is a reference to the Bubonic plague that afflicted Europe in the 14th century and resulted in the deaths of countless people.

Example #10

"Gallop apace, you fiery-footed steeds,
Towards Phoebus' lodging. Such a wagoner
As Phaëton would whip you to the west
And bring in cloudy night immediately."
(III.ii. 1-4)

While expressing her impatience for reuniting with Romeo, Juliet alludes to Phaeton's chariot in the above lines. According to Greek mythology, Phaeton was the son of Phoebus, the sun god. One day Phaeton asked his father that he be allowed to ride the sun chariot. Phoebus agreed, but unfortunately, Phaeton could not control the horses, and they rushed across the sky. Juliet wishes for a rider as fast as Phaeton to emerge across the sky so that night would approach quickly thus ensuring Juliet's much-anticipated meeting with Romeo.

CHAPTER II

Dramatic Irony in Hamlet

Dramatic Irony is a form of irony which is a literary device. Shakespeare employs it in his works masterfully. It happens when the audience knows more than the events and the world of the play more than those characters in that play. It involves the whole structure of the work.

In the play Hamlet, a few major characters' awareness of their situation is critically different from that of the reader. Therefore, their actions go in contradiction to what the readers may be anticipating. It turns the whole work very engaging for the readers. It enhances their emotional participation in the play.

In the very first Act of the play, the ghost of Hamlet's father reveals to him that his death was not due to what everyone might be thinking of rather it was the betrayal of Claudius who poured poison into his ear when he was asleep.

Now, this knowledge isn't known to all major characters Hamlet interact with but his friends, and the audience and himself. Here the dramatic irony is the clash of Hamlet's actions aware of that knowledge with the actions of for example Gertrude, Polonius, Laertes and Claudius himself who doesn't know in the beginning that Hamlet already knows the truth of his crimes.

Hamlet jostles across all these and it results in his delay from taking revenge for his father's death. In the third Act of the play, Polonius admits his crime when he says, *"my offence is rank, it smells to heaven; It hath the primal eldest curse upon't, a brother's murder."*

It is the knowledge known to the only audience but Claudius doesn't know that Hamlet knows it about him and Hamlet knows that Claudius doesn't know that it has already been revealed to him. It is a situation where multi-layered dramatic irony is working.

Hence, we see that Claudius feels like he can't pray because of the graveness of his crime and Hamlet thinks of not killing him while he is praying because it may send him to heaven which he doesn't want. In the same Act, Hamlet visits his mother Gertrude, the queen.

Only the audience and the queen know that Polonius who was talking to her earlier is hiding behind the tapestry. When Hamlet successfully unnerves Gertrude, it threatens her composure, it reveals her true character and she shouts for help and Hamlet sensing someone behind the tapestry, mistakes it for Claudius and stabs Polonius and he dies.

The whole engaging power of this scene is due to this dramatic irony which helps contrasting out the coming tragedy in the plot. In the last Act of the play, Claudius pursues Laertes successfully into a fencing match and convinces Hamlet to take part in it too.

Here, both of them plot against him by dipping Laertes' sword into poison so that Hamlet dies in the match and as a backup plan Claudius has poisoned the wine kept on the table which will kill Hamlet nevertheless but the dramatic irony is that Hamlet and Gertrude are unaware of it.

Dramatically, their sword gets exchanged, both of them die and before the queen sips from the wine unknowingly and dies. The truth about Claudius is revealed. Laertes makes it up with Hamlet but the whole scene is so engaging because certain characters' knowledge isn't known to certain other characters.

It makes it just like life where we can only know the motive behind our own actions and hardly that of others. Hamlet's plot employs Dramatic Irony that brilliantly.

Dramatic Irony in Shakespeare's Othello

The element of dramatic irony is very striking in the play Othello. There is always a great gap between what many things appear to be and what they really are. There is irony in the gap between the appearance and reality of Iago's personality, and there is also a mind-disturbing irony in the way Othello always believes the false and never believes the true.

William Shakespeare (1564-1616)

As always, the dramatic irony in the play lies in the action or speech of the characters who speak or act that way because they wrongly understand the reality or situation. Othello, who has so gullibly believed Iago the villain, misunderstands the way his loving wife Desdemona takes his love and her love for granted and talks about Cassio so honestly. Desdemona is too innocent, and she talks in an irritating manner about Cassio's case when the husband is so disturbed; it is so ironical that she tries to please her angry husband with something that adds fuel to the fire of his anger. Cassio is always mistaken in his understanding of the situation; his actions and speech are all ironical as when he requests Iago to help him, when in fact Iago is planning to ruin him.

Roderigo is the fourth gullible fool to become the victim of Iago, but without understanding that he is so systematically ruined by Iago he trusts him more than anyone else. And finally, the 'curse' given to Othello while giving the blessings by Brabantio is one of the most terrible ironies in the drama; the old man tells Othello to be careful because Desdemona may betray her husband as she has betrayed her father! And this comes out 'true', to the mind of the foolish tragic hero. Another unconscious irony is in Othello's speech when he meets Desdemona just after he arrives from the sea. He says that he is so overjoyed by her presence and company that he is afraid that the bliss may end so soon due to some unknown fate. And this is what happens very soon.

Besides the 'dramatic' irony when we are conscious about the reality and the character is acting or speaking on the basis of a misunderstanding, there are also many instances of 'verbal' irony when a character consciously satirizes, insults or teases another character. This is usually done by Iago, who insults and teases Roderigo and Cassio and even Desdemona and Othello. Those poor gullible characters do not understand the actual meaning and the insult but we understand it. For instance, just before Brabantio is brought to the scene by Roderigo, lago seems to be talking in favor of Othello and against Brabantio. He says that he wanted to kill the old man because he talked badly against Othello's honor. But his intention is evil; he wants to ruin Othello by separating his just married wife Desdemona. Similarly, he used ironical and spiteful language when he talks about Desdemona in act 2 scene I. Even his soliloquies are ironical, but at times we are struck by the power of his verbal ironies, as when he teases Othello by saying that "Men must be what they seem to be"!

Like the dramatic and verbal irony, there is also what is called the irony of fate in this play. Othello suffers from that irony of fate because chances lead him to the disaster and he finds out every truth too late. But the other characters are also victims of the irony of fate. Desdemona is innocent, except that she is guilty of being too innocent, and is unaware of the evil traps of her world, but she is victimized by her destiny. Similarly, Cassio also suffers without being evil or doing anything bad, again except being too simple-minded. And Roderigo and Emilia also suffer the same irony of fate.

Romeo and Juliet

Dramatic Irony

Dramatic irony is a literary device commonly used by playwrights in their plays. It occurs when the audience understands the implication and significance of a specific situation on stage, whereas the characters are unaware of the gravity of the meanings underlying that situation.

Characterized as one of the hallmarks of Shakespearean tragedies, dramatic irony is used to build and sustain audience's interest thereby keeping them actively engaged in the play. Some of its examples in "Romeo and Juliet" are given below with analysis.

Dramatic Irony in *Romeo and Juliet*

Example #1:

pair of star-cross'd lovers take their life... (Prologue 6)

The aforementioned verse, taken from the prologue, highlights the first instance of dramatic irony in the play. In this line, the chorus asserts that the play about is going to revolve around two lovers who commit suicide.

The irony resides in the fact that this tragic end is revealed to the audience but not to the characters involved in it. Thus, from the outset, the audience becomes aware that Romeo and Juliet's love is destined to fail whereas the main characters remain oblivious to this fact.

Example #2:

Whose misadventur'd piteous overthrows

Doth, with their death, bury their parents' strife. (Prologue 7-8)

The above revelation is made by the chorus in the prologue of the play. Referring to the deaths of the two passionate lovers, the chorus emphasizes that the legacy of rivalry between the Capulets and Montagues will only end after the tragic deaths of their children, Romeo and Juliet.

The irony is inherent in the fact that the unfortunate deaths of two lovers will bring about a peaceful resolution to an otherwise long-standing conflict between their families. The irony is further intensified by the fact that while the audience is aware of it, the two rival families remain obstinately unaware of the consequences of their animosity.

Example #3:

This holy shrine, the gentle fine is this:
My lips, two blushing pilgrims, ready stand
To smooth that rough touch with a tender kiss. (I.v. 105-107)

These heartfelt lines are uttered by a love-struck Romeo who regards himself as an ardent pilgrim and Juliet as his scared shrine. As a self-professed and devoted pilgrim, Romeo pleads that he be allowed to kiss his holy shrine. The ironic fact about the entire wooing incident is that at this stage Romeo is not aware that Juliet is the daughter of the Capulets, his family's archrivals. Thus, he unknowingly falls in love with his nemesis.

Example #4:

Alack, there lies more peril in thine eye
Than twenty of their swords! Look thou but sweet,
And I am proof against their enmity. (II. ii. 76-78)

These lines are uttered by Romeo to Juliet in the renowned balcony scene. In these particular verses, Romeo is trying to reassure Juliet that she needs not worry about her family issuing threats to him. Moreover, Romeo tries to convince Juliet that her sweet and loving gaze will protect him from all dangers.

Romeo is confident that their love will win against all odds. Yet, the audience is aware that Juliet's fears are not unfounded. In fact, nothing can protect the young lovers from their doomed romance.

Example #5:

Alas poor Romeo! he is already dead;
stabbed with a white wench's black eye;
shot through the ear with a love-song; (II. iv. 14-16)

The aforementioned remarks are made by Mercutio while he is conversing with Benvolio. The conversation revolves around Romeo's love-stricken state. The irony resides in the fact that whereas both Mercutio and Benvolio assume that Romeo is craving for Rosaline, the audience is aware that reality is contrary to their perception, and that Juliet is the newfound center of Romeo's love and affection.

Example #6:

Ah, well-a-day! he's dead, he's dead, he's dead!
We are undone, lady, we are undone!
Alack the day! he's gone, he's kill'd, he's dead! (III. ii. 42-44)

Juliet's nurse delivers the aforementioned disturbing news in relation to Tybalt's death. The nurse only used the pronoun "he" to describe who died. Juliet thought that the nurse was referring to Romeo. She thought that he has been killed. This has made her become engulfed in sadness. As opposed to Juliet, the audience is aware that Romeo is still alive which exacerbates the dramatic irony underlying the situation.

Example #7:

Where I have learn'd me to repent the sin
Of disobedient opposition
To you and your behests, and am enjoin'd

By holy Laurence to fall prostrate here,
And beg your pardon… (IV.ii. 18-22)

Juliet makes the above-mentioned earnest remarks in an effort to give her father the impression that she is a dutiful daughter who harbors no intention to contest her parents' wishes. Although Juliet's feigned earnestness convinces her father that she has happily conceded to marry Paris, the reality is that she is only pretending to be an obedient, respectful daughter.

The audience is aware that Juliet has already made a prior plan with the Friar to drink the sleeping potion and has no intention of marrying Paris. This contrast between Capulet's naiveté and the actual truth known by the audience, contributes to the dramatic irony and tension of the scene.

Example #8:

If I may trust the flattering truth of sleep,
My dreams presage some joyful news at hand. (V. i. 1-2)

Uttered by Romeo, the aforementioned verse is replete with manifold layers of dramatic irony. The first instance of irony resides in the fact that although Romeo anticipates joyful news, moments later Balthasar ushers in and delivers the news of Juliet's death.

This terrible news leads Romeo to commit suicide. Romeo does not know the ultimate reason why Juliet has committed suicide. He did not know what drove Juliet in order to do this act. Out of his love, he decided to follow and commit suicide too.

Example #9:

I could not send it,- here it is again, -
Nor get a messenger to bring it thee,
So fearful were they of infection. (V. ii. 14-16)

Friar John made these remarks in response to Friar Laurence's inquiry about the letter supposedly dispatched to Romeo. Romeo is supposed to be informed of Juliet's plan to take the sleeping potion to escape her marriage. However, the above revelation by Friar John highlights that plague outbreak made him unable to deliver the letter to Romeo.

The irony is inherent in the fact that due to this failure to deliver the letter, Romeo stays unaware of the fact that Juliet is alive – a fact that would have otherwise saved his life.

Example #10:

Ah, dear Juliet,
Why art thou yet so fair? shall I believe
That unsubstantial death is amorous,
And that the lean abhorred monster keeps
Thee here in dark to be his paramour?
For fear of that, I still will stay with thee;
And never from this palace of dim night... (V. iii. 101-107)

Romeo uttered these lines when he saw Juliet lying in the tomb. The dramatic irony implicit in the aforementioned verses evokes sympathy in the audience. Overwhelmed by his love for Juliet, Romeo makes a pledge to join his beloved in the dim night of death. The fact that Juliet appears beautiful and utterly untouched by death highlights the dramatic irony underlying this tragic scene, since Juliet is actually sound asleep and not dead.

CHAPTER III

Analysis of Hamlet's Soliloquies in Acts I, II, and III

Shakespeare's soliloquies give the reader, or the audience, the opportunity to witness what is going on in a character's mind. While these soliloquies are, of course, spoken by the characters, they offer the reader some insight into Shakespeare's concerns about the human condition.

Soliloquies Covered in This Article

- Act 1. Scene 2: *'Oh that this too solid flesh would melt...'*
- Act 2. Scene 2: *'Now I am alone. O, what a rogue and peasant slave am I!...'*
- Act 3. Scene 1: *'To be, or not to be...'*

Hamlet's Soliloquy, Act 1. Scene II

O, that this too too solid flesh would melt
Thaw and resolve itself into a dew!
Or that the Everlasting had not fix'd
His canon 'gainst self-slaughter! O God! God!
How weary, stale, flat and unprofitable,
Seem to me all the uses of this world!
Fie on't! ah fie! 'tis an unweeded garden,
That grows to seed; things rank and gross in nature
Possess it merely. That it should come to this!
But two months dead: nay, not so much, not two:

So excellent a king; that was, to this,
Hyperion to a satyr; so loving to my mother
That he might not beteem the winds of heaven
Visit her face too roughly. Heaven and earth!
Must I remember? why, she would hang on him,
As if increase of appetite had grown
By what it fed on: and yet, within a month –
Let me not think on't – Frailty, thy name is woman! –
A little month, or ere those shoes were old
With which she follow'd my poor father's body,
Like Niobe, all tears: – why she, even she –
O, God! a beast, that wants discourse of reason,
Would have mourn'd longer – married with my uncle,
My father's brother, but no more like my father
Than I to Hercules: within a month:
Ere yet the salt of most unrighteous tears
Had left the flushing in her galled eyes,
She married. O, most wicked speed, to post
With such dexterity to incestuous sheets!
It is not nor it cannot come to good:
But break, my heart; for I must hold my tongue.

Analysis of Hamlet's Soliloquy, Act 1. Scene II

This soliloquy begins with Hamlet desiring death, saying, 'this too solid flesh would melt', but this desire comes coupled with the fear that God does not condone 'self-slaughter'. This reveals that Hamlet is feeling melancholic. It's possible that he is suffering from depression. Apart from desiring suicide, he also states that he is finding the world 'weary, stale, flat and unprofitable'. This is more proof that Hamlet is depressed. However, depression does not come absent other emotions.

As we read further, we find that Hamlet's depression leads to bitterness and disgust. This is most apparent when Hamlet describes the world as 'rank', 'gross', and 'unweeded'.

Hamlet's growing sense of melancholy and disgust is a result of two horrific events. First, his father, the king, died less than two months prior to Hamlet's soliloquy. Hamlet is grieving for his father, whom he honoured and loved, comparing him to 'Hyperion'.

Second, his mother, who should be sharing his grief, has betrayed his needs and his father's memory. She has celebrated a hasty and unseemly marriage to the old king's brother, Claudius. Hamlet's distress and disgust are illustrated in his comment, 'a beast that wants of reason would have mourned longer'. Here, we see that Hamlet feels as though his mother has sullied his father's memory saying, 'Frailty, thy name is woman'. The matter torments him so much that he can hardly bear to consider it. 'Must I remember?' he asks in desperation, then he says, 'Let me not think on't'.

He is not only shocked and upset by the haste with which his mother has decided to remarry, but he is also disgusted by the husband she has chosen. Because she marries her dead husband's brother, Claudius, Hamlet believes that she is committing incest. Hamlet dislikes Claudius, whom he compares to a 'satyr'. Hamlet despises being called Claudius's 'son'. While he agrees to 'obey' his mother's wishes, he mocks Claudius's irritating comments. It is obvious that Hamlet cannot stomach seeing Claudius in such a high position of power.

It is likely that he may also feel that his own place has been usurped. He has not inherited his father's crown, but rather, it is now worn by Claudius. This renders Hamlet powerless. Hamlet is convinced that this unfortunate situation 'cannot come to good', but feels impotent. How can Hamlet lead his country and honor his father's death when such a malicious buffoon sits on the throne?

He feels depressed, suicidal, fearful, regretful, grief-stricken, angry, disgusted, betrayed, frustrated, confused and impotent. His thoughts are of death and decay. This speech indicates the level of negativity to which Hamlet has fallen. He is haunted by his father's death, tormented by his mother's marriage to Claudius, and infuriated by his inability to change either event.

Hamlet's Soliloquy, Act 2. Scene II

Now I am alone.
O, what a rogue and peasant slave am I!
Is it not monstrous that this player here,
But in a fiction, in a dream of passion,
Could force his soul so to his own conceit
That from her working all his visage wann'd,
Tears in his eyes, distraction in's aspect,
A broken voice, and his whole function suiting
With forms to his conceit? and all for nothing!
For Hecuba!
What's Hecuba to him, or he to Hecuba,
That he should weep for her? What would he do,
Had he the motive and the cue for passion
That I have? He would drown the stage with tears
And cleave the general ear with horrid speech,
Make mad the guilty and appal the free,
Confound the ignorant, and amaze indeed
The very faculties of eyes and ears. Yet I,
A dull and muddy-mettled rascal, peak,
Like John-a-dreams, unpregnant of my cause,
And can say nothing; no, not for a king,
Upon whose property and most dear life
A damn'd defeat was made. Am I a coward?
Who calls me villain? breaks my pate across?
Plucks off my beard, and blows it in my face?
Tweaks me by the nose? gives me the lie i' the throat,
As deep as to the lungs? who does me this?
Ha!
'Swounds, I should take it: for it cannot be
But I am pigeon-liver'd and lack gall
To make oppression bitter, or ere this
I should have fatted all the region kites
With this slave's offal: bloody, bawdy villain!
Remorseless, treacherous, lecherous, kindless villain!
O, vengeance!
Why, what an ass am I! This is most brave,

That I, the son of a dear father murder'd,
Prompted to my revenge by heaven and hell,
Must, like a whore, unpack my heart with words,
And fall a-cursing, like a very drab,
A scullion!
Fie upon't! foh! About, my brain! I have heard
That guilty creatures sitting at a play
Have by the very cunning of the scene
Been struck so to the soul that presently
They have proclaim'd their malefactions;
For murder, though it have no tongue, will speak
With most miraculous organ. I'll have these players
Play something like the murder of my father
Before mine uncle: I'll observe his looks;
I'll tent him to the quick: if he but blench,
I know my course. The spirit that I have seen
May be the devil: and the devil hath power
To assume a pleasing shape; yea, and perhaps
Out of my weakness and my melancholy,
As he is very potent with such spirits,
Abuses me to damn me: I'll have grounds
More relative than this: the play 's the thing
Wherein I'll catch the conscience of the king.

Analysis of Hamlet's Soliloquy, Act 2. Scene II

This soliloquy illustrates Hamlet's continued inability to do anything of consequence. He lacks the knowledge of how to remedy the pain caused by his present circumstances, so he wonders how an actor would portray him, saying, '[he would] drown the stage with tears'. One has to assume that this is what Hamlet wants to do, and what he feels his father's death deserves, yet he is unable to respond in this way. He wonders if he is a coward, since he does not 'cleave the general ear with horrid speech' or 'make mad the guilty and appal the free'. He asks, 'who calls me villain?', but the only person speaking is himself. At this point, he is accusing himself of villainy for not speaking on behalf of his dear, recently-deceased, father.

He believes that he must be a 'pigeon-liver'd' coward, lacking 'gall', because he does not do anything about the 'bloody, bawdy villain', Claudius. He wants revenge on his 'remorseless, treacherous, lecherous, kindless', uncle, but he can only complain to himself and accomplish nothing. He criticises his own inaction, calling himself 'scullion', 'whore', and 'drab' for not doing more in respect of his father's death; for saying nothing about a king, 'upon whose property and most dear life a damned defeat was made'; for not killing Claudius and 'feeding his innards to the kites'.

However, his feelings settle some when Hamlet remembers that a play, reflecting the murder of Old Hamlet, by Claudius, might cause the latter to react in such a way as to prove his guilt. He needs this evidence because he worries that the ghost that he has spoken with could turn out to be 'a devil', luring him, in his weak and melancholy state, to commit a sin against his possibly innocent uncle. The play, which he plans with the acting troupe, will give him the answers that he requires.

Hamlet still feels grief-stricken, frustrated and angry, but his impotent and confused cowardice is being overcome by a belief that he can do something about his situation.

Hamlet's Soliloquy, Act 3. Scene I

To be, or not to be: that is the question:
Whether 'tis nobler in the mind to suffer
The slings and arrows of outrageous fortune,
Or to take arms against a sea of troubles,
And by opposing end them? To die: to sleep;
No more; and by a sleep to say we end
The heart-ache and the thousand natural shocks
That flesh is heir to, 'tis a consummation
Devoutly to be wish'd. To die, to sleep;
To sleep: perchance to dream: ay, there's the rub;
For in that sleep of death what dreams may come
When we have shuffled off this mortal coil,
Must give us pause: there's the respect
That makes calamity of so long life;

For who would bear the whips and scorns of time,
The oppressor's wrong, the proud man's contumely,
The pangs of despised love, the law's delay,
The insolence of office and the spurns
That patient merit of the unworthy takes,
When he himself might his quietus make
With a bare bodkin? who would fardels bear,
To grunt and sweat under a weary life,
But that the dread of something after death,
The undiscover'd country from whose bourn
No traveller returns, puzzles the will
And makes us rather bear those ills we have
Than fly to others that we know not of?
Thus conscience does make cowards of us all;
And thus the native hue of resolution
Is sicklied o'er with the pale cast of thought,
And enterprises of great pith and moment
With this regard their currents turn awry,
And lose the name of action.

Analysis of Hamlet's Soliloquy, Act 3. Scene I

Hamlet's third soliloquy is the famous 'to be, or not to be' speech. Once again Hamlet is confused and contemplating death. He is wondering whether life or death is preferable; whether it is better to allow himself to be tormented by all the wrongs that he considers 'outrageous fortune' bestowed on him, or to arm himself and fight against them, bringing them to an end. If he were to die, he feels that his troubles, his 'heart-ache', would end. Death is still something that he finds appealing, 'tis a consummation devoutly to be wished'. Yet, even death troubles him, as to die might mean to dream and he worries about the dreams he might have to endure, 'in that sleep of death what dreams may come'.

He is still contemplating suicide and considers how, by taking one's own life, with 'a bare bodkin', or dagger, one might avoid 'whips and scorns' and other hard-to-bear wrongs. However, he refers to death as 'the dread of something' in the 'undiscover'd country', and this shows that he worried about how his soul might be treated in the afterlife.

He decides that fears concerning the puzzling and 'dreadful' afterlife, together with the conscience, cause people to bear the wrongs inflicted during their life on earth, rather than commit suicide and risk offending God. The fear of arriving somewhere unknown and frightening—possibly the torments of hell—is proof that 'conscience does make cowards of us all'. People, he concludes, tend to think things over, lack resolve and do nothing.

When Hamlet is remarking on such people, he is actually talking about himself. He believes that his uncle is wicked and deserves to die. He believes that it is he who should end his uncle's life. But he is afraid of going to purgatory, as the spirit claiming to be his father has done. He is afraid of risking hell by committing suicide. He is afraid of doing the wrong thing, and is inactive, partly because of his conscience. He is afraid of the potential consequences that his religious upbringing—an upbringing that would have been the norm—claim would come if he commits suicide.

Hamlet continues to feel frustrated and angry in his grief, and his feelings of impotence have returned. Although Claudius's response to the play indicated guilt, Hamlet still does not know what the right thing to do is—right in the eyes of God, that is.

Similarities in Hamlet's Three Soliloquies

All three speeches illustrate a man, confused and wracked by grief, wanting revenge, but not knowing how to go about responding to what has happened. He is uncertain of his own feelings and how to cope with them. He feels weak, melancholic and powerless. He does not know what the right thing to do is, or how to do it. In all three soliloquies, Hamlet is struggling to make sense of his overwhelming grief.

Important Soliloquies in Othello

William Shakespeare, the best playwright, author, actor and poet of perpetuity, has constantly used soliloquies in his plays. There is just small distinction between soliloquies and monologues, and mainly these terms are interchangeable. In reality, if making the material analysis of Shakespeare's plays, it is evident that he enjoys using soliloquies. Probably, this choice came out of the desire and need to emphasize the inner thoughts that have been prowling in his character's minds, therefore, giving the audience an insight into some vital details. In simple words, you'll discover numerous soliloquies in Othello, due to the fact that they assisted Shakespeare establish and own the plot and the character appropriately.

For instance, when Iago pronounces words such as "I am not exactly what I am", it displays the honesty of the character, it assists to highlight the intricacy of his figure in this play, and to provoke wider understanding of the dramatic predicament.

In Act I, Scene iii and Act II, Scene I, it can easily be seen exactly what Iago's self-interest is and how the misinterpretation of scenarios has led him to the choice about the requirement of vengeance, and finally to nearly clinical fixation. These soliloquies expose Iago's intentions, and frustrating desire to take revenge by controlling Othello and taking advantage of Othello's open nature.

In Act I, Scene iii, 393, the soliloquy "I know his trumpet" delivered by Iago where "his" relates to Othello, clarifies that Iago knows the weak points of Othello, and he intends to utilize his jealousy versus Othello himself. He does this by misinforming Othello about his Desdemona having an affair with Cassio, a worthy lieutenant under Othello's command and a buddy of Desdemona. As the story plays along, the audience realizes that Lago is enjoying his complete satisfaction for vengeance, which can be seen in his soliloquy in Act II, Scene iii. In this soliloquy, the audience then gets to know Iago's developing plan and how quickly it has actually been for him to use Cassio and Roderigo for his wicked obtain.

In Act III, Scene iii; we can see how Othello has actually been crippled by Iago's deceit when he utilizes the soliloquy, "for I am black," which shows his insecurities and doubts. Listening to this dramatic speech, we can see that Othello has a hard time over his faith in his wife, Desdemona.

In Act V, Scene ii, it can be plainly perceived how Iago's deceptiveness has actually led Othello to believing that his other half has actually been having an affair with Cassio behind his back. The idea of being tricked was so striking that Othello chose to eliminate the love of his life. Verbally, in the "betray more males" soliloquy, Othello describes his decision not with the allusions to his love or pain, however with the intention to avoid Desdemona from deceiving other male. Till now there are hot conversations around the honesty of those claims.

Nevertheless, in the last soliloquies, "so sweet was ne'er so fatal" and "oculus proof", it is confirmed that Othello has actually been defeated by the over-riding impacts and misleading control of Lago. Shakespeare, known for his soliloquies, uses them to make sure that the audience understands exactly what's happening with the plot and to keep them informed about the character's objective, which is what has made his plays so interesting to check out.

Without the use of these soliloquies, it would have been practically impossible to let the audience know exactly what's happening inside of the terrible hero's' soul, without interfering with the characters or play.

By now, you should have pretty good idea on how you must start and how an analytical essay on Othello must be composed. However naturally, you do not wish to write some mediocre paper, you wish to compose something that can catch the attention of your professor or teacher, and leave him astonished.

Romeo And Juliet Soliloquy

Within a dramatic play, an insightful monologue that conveys a character's inner feelings, viewpoints and thoughts are referred to as a soliloquy. Regarded as an essential dramatic device, a soliloquy is delivered by a character who is alone on the stage. In most Elizabethan tragedies and especially in Shakespearean plays, a soliloquy offers key insights into the mind of a certain character.

The soliloquies featured in "Romeo and Juliet" are detailed and delivered with passionate intensity. These soliloquies add complexity and depth to various characters thereby magnifying their life-like appeal. Moreover, the riveting and heart-rending disclosure made by Romeo, Juliet, Juliet's nurse and other characters in certain soliloquies, draws the audience to feel profound empathy for these characters. Some of the soliloquies are discussed below:

Soliloquy in "Romeo and Juliet"

Example #1

"But soft, what light through yonder window breaks?
It is the East, and Juliet is the sun.
Arise, fair sun, and kill the envious moon,
Who is already sick and pale with grief
That thou, her maid, art far more fair than she."
(II. ii. 7-11)

This soliloquy is delivered by Romeo during the balcony scene. After his initial meeting with Juliet at the Capulet ball, Romeo spends hours yearning for her and eagerly waiting to reunite with her. This soliloquy highlights Romeo's abundant love and admiration for Juliet. After seeing Juliet standing by her window, Romeo is overwhelmed by his love for her and regards Juliet as being more beautiful than the ascending sun. He further claims that the moon is grief-stricken and envious because Juliet is infinite times more beautiful than the moon.

Example #2

"What's in a name? That which we call a rose
By any other word would smell as sweet.
So Romeo would, were he not Romeo called,
Retain that dear perfection which he owes
Without that title."
(II. ii. 46- 50)

This passionate soliloquy is delivered by Juliet during the balcony scene. Intense, eloquent and infused with emotion, this beautiful and oft-quoted soliloquy makes the audience aware of the true depth of Juliet's feelings for Romeo. Dismissing and trivializing the significance of a name, Juliet passionately maintains that the essence and fragrance of a rose would remain unchanged disregard for a change in its name. Likewise, Juliet's beloved Romeo would remain equally untainted and precious if he were addressed by any other name.

Example #3

"For naught so vile that on the Earth doth live
But to the Earth some special good doth give;
Nor aught so good but, strained from that fair use,
Revolts from true birth, stumbling on abuse."
(II. iii. 17-20)

This soliloquy is delivered by Friar Lawrence to highlight the essential function of everything existing in this world. In his preacher-like tone, Friar Lawrence emphatically maintains that nothing inhabiting this earth can be deemed evil because the earth does derive some sort of benefit from it. The Friar also highlights the duality of good asserting that everything perceived good also has an inherent destructive element. The significant lesson implicit in this soliloquy is that both good and evil have the tendency to transform into their respective antithesis.

Example #4

"The clock struck nine when I did send the Nurse.
In half an hour she promised to return.

Perchance she cannot meet him. That's not so.
O, she is lame! Love's heralds should be thoughts,
Which ten times faster glides than the sun's beams"
(II. v. 1-5)

This particular soliloquy is delivered by Juliet while she is eagerly waiting for her nurse's return. Juliet says that although the nurse promised to return by nine-thirty after meeting Romeo, she has not returned as expected. Anxious, Juliet entertains the idea that the nurse was perhaps unable to meet Romeo and confirm if he actually wants to marry Juliet. Abruptly dismissing this idea the next instant, Juliet states that the nurse is probably slow and that love's messengers should be faster than the sun's beams. This soliloquy highlights Juliet's impatience in terms of confirming her highly anticipated marital bond with Romeo.

Example #5

"Come, gentle night; come, loving black-browed night,
Give me my Romeo, and when I shall die,
Take him and cut him out in little stars,
And he will make the face of heaven so fine
That all the world will be in love with night..."
(III. ii. 18-23)

In this particular soliloquy, Juliet professes her love for Romeo once again. While waiting for her much-awaited union with Romeo, Juliet invokes the night, asking it to hasten its arrival. She further states that if Romeo were to be cut up in little stars after his death, he would brighten the sky with his unprecedented beauty. This soliloquy reflects Juliet's immense adoration for Romeo.

Example #6

"Farewell.—God knows when we shall meet again.
I have a faint cold fear thrills through my veins
That almost freezes up the heat of life.
I'll call them back again to comfort me.—

Nurse!—What should she do here?
My dismal scene I needs must act alone."
(IV. iii. 15-20)

This soliloquy is spoken by Juliet, moments prior to her drinking the sleeping potion. The detailed, passionate quote reflects Juliet's fear about the outcome of her plan. She bids farewell to her loved ones exclaiming that she does not know when they will meet again. She then acknowledges the chilling fear that runs down her spine and wonders if she should ask her nurse to comfort her. Juliet then immediately dismisses this thought and asserts that she must carry out her dismal plan of drinking the potion herself.

Example #7

"Mistress! What, mistress! Juliet!—Fast, I warrant her, she—
Why, lamb, why, lady! Fie, you slugabed!
Why, love, I say! Madam! Sweetheart! Why, bride!—
What, not a word?"
(IV. v. 1-5)

This soliloquy is delivered by Juliet's nurse after she sees Juliet deeply asleep in her bed and mistakenly perceives her as being dead. After using several terms of endearment for Juliet in an effort to wake her up, the nurse becomes slightly anxious when Juliet is completely unresponsive. The nurse's frightful reaction makes the audience aware of the fact that she is not aware of the plan formulated by Juliet and Friar Lawrence.

Example #8

"I dreamt my lady came and found me dead
(Strange dream that gives a dead man leave to think!)
And breathed such life with kisses in my lips
That I revived and was an emperor."
(V. i. 6-10)

This significant soliloquy is uttered by Romeo and serves as a prelude to the events that unfold in the following scenes. Romeo says that he had a dream in which his beloved Juliet found him dead and kissed him as a result of which, he was brought back to life and became an emperor. This particular monologue of Romeo is heard only by the audience and serves as a testament to the fact that a mere dream of Juliet has the power to rekindle hope and joy in Romeo. Thus, Juliet is Romeo's lifeline in a way.

Example #9

"Sweet flower, with flowers thy bridal bed I strew
(O woe, thy canopy is dust and stones!)
Which with sweet water nightly I will dew,
Or, wanting that, with tears distilled by moans.
The obsequies that I for thee will keep
Nightly shall be to strew thy grave and weep."
(V. iii. 12-17)

This heartfelt soliloquy is delivered by Paris while he is scattering flowers near Juliet's tomb. This soliloquy delineates Paris' immense love and reverence for Juliet. By exclaiming that he will either water the flowers scattered near Juliet's tomb every night or hold a special ritual in her remembrance and weep for her daily. Paris is able to evoke sympathy from the audience. It is primarily because of this soliloquy the audience is able to dismantle the previously held cold and aloof image of Paris.

Example #10

"He told me Paris should have married Juliet.
Said he not so? Or did I dream it so?
Or am I mad, hearing him talk of Juliet,
To think it was so?—O, give me thy hand,
One writ with me in sour misfortune's book!"
(V. iii. 78- 82)

This soliloquy delivered by Romeo is replete with remorse and is spoken moments after Romeo's senseless killing of Count

Paris. After identifying Paris as his victim, Romeo remorsefully reflects on whether his servant had informed him of Paris' plan of marrying Juliet and whether this information had subconsciously led him to kill Paris. Unable to think clearly, Romeo entertains the notion that perhaps his servant said no such thing and he merely dreamt it. Thereafter, in a state of agonizing regret, Romeo addresses Paris' body and sadly exclaims that both he and Romeo are similar in terms of experiencing bad fortune. This insightful soliloquy emphasizes Romeo's guilt and remorse thereby redeeming him in the eyes of the audience.

CHAPTER IV

HAMLET SYMBOLISM

Symbolism means an artistic and poetic expression or style using figurative images and indirect ideas to express mystical ideas, emotions, and states of mind. The reader will find significant symbolism thought the play 'Hamlet' which shows a variety of connotations from situation to situation and context to context. Some of the most important symbols in Hamlet are discussed below.

Symbolism in Hamlet

Symbol #1

Ghost

The appearance of the ghost of Old Hamlet in the very first scene of the play symbolizes tough times are coming ahead. It signifies the presence of supernatural powers like the three witches of Macbeth. However, it represents the difficult times ahead for Hamlet as well as Claudius, making the revelation that Claudius is the murderer of Old Hamlet. Ghost also symbolizes the foreshadow of the upcoming the turmoil in Denmark as Hamlet prepares to take revenge against Claudius. It shows that the ghost is not a good but a bad omen for the state of Denmark as well as its ruler, Claudius.

Symbol #2

Flowers

Flowers appear in Hamlet when Ophelia loses her mind. She starts distributing flowers to everybody she meets. She presents each flower, describing what it stands for and then moves to the next. The flowers show various features as she states that rosemary is for remembrance, pansy for thoughts and so on. Ophelia expresses her pain of the betrayal she felt by offering the flowers and describing what they symbolize. Her father's murder and Hamlet's taunt takes its toll on her. That is why the flowers symbolize her inner turmoil and also her faithfulness.

Symbol #3

Skull

The skull in Hamlet is of Yorick, the court's jester. This skull is a symbol of death, decay and uselessness of a person after his death. It is a physical remnant of the dead person that is an omen of what he may have to face in the life hereafter. The skull makes Hamlet think about his own destiny and his own life after his death. It implies how man finally returns to dust. The skull reminds Hamlet that even "Imperious Caesar" is subject to death and decay. Death does not leave anybody intact or alive.

Symbol #4

Weather

Weather is another important symbol in Hamlet. It shows that the bad weather is the sign of worse situation coming ahead and good weather points to good times. However, in the first scene, Shakespeare has shown that the weather is frigid and foggy in which the ghost of Old Hamlet appears. This confusing and ambivalent weather is signifying the same situation coming ahead. Hamlet is confused like the situation that is hazy and unclear. Therefore, the good or bad weather is the sign of good or bad times in the play.

Symbol #5

Graveyard

Although death is in the mind of Hamlet since the play starts, it becomes an important subject when he enters the graveyard. The gravedigger plays with words when responding to Hamlet's questions. He gives him the philosophy of life that all sort of skulls whether they are of the kings or beggars are lying there in the graveyard. He responds that all the dead persons are equal when they are stripped of their political statuses. Graveyard signifies a place where all are equal and the people working in the graveyards become insensitive to the positions and political status of the dead.

Symbol #6

The Mousetrap

The Mousetrap is the play titled as The Murder of Gonzago, which has been staged in Hamlet. Hamlet has given directions to the players and written parts of the speech delivered by the queen. The title 'The Mousetrap' shows that the purpose of Hamlet to insert his own ideas in the play to force his mother to confess her crime, recall her promise to her late husband or at least show signs of guilt. It is also interesting that almost all the characters in this short play are based on the real characters who are watching them on the stage. Therefore, the story is symbolical for the trap laid by Hamlet to catch the real culprit.

Symbol #7

Fencing Swords

Fencing swords in Hamlet have been used in the final scene during the duel between Laertes and Hamlet. The fencing swords point to the approach of the end of Hamlet's quest and resultant deaths. The fencing sword is a sign of a person having courage, bravery and the will to exact revenge. As both the characters engaged in fencing swords have some cause, and also have their honors at stake, they come to fight a duel in which both are killed. Therefore, fencing swords symbolize violence and deaths in the play.

Symbol #8

Gravedigger

Although there are two gravediggers, one of them is not only a good player of words but also a good philosopher. His responses to the questions posed by Hamlet show that he knows how death makes all equal in the graveyard. He also knows that he has dug graves of everyone who died. When digging Ophelia's grave, they also point out to Hamlet that it doesn't matter whether somebody has committed suicide. Their presence signifies that deaths make all people equal in spite of their positions.

Symbol #9

Hamlet's costume changes

Throughout the play, Hamlet wears dark blue cloak to express his mourning for his dead father. As the days pass, his mother insists him to stop mourning. However, Hamlet continues to wear black clothes that keep him apart. It symbolizes that Hamlet doesn't care about outward appearance and wanted to remember his father until he seeks revenge. Hamlet's black costume shows his anguish.

Symbol #10

Poison

Poison is a recurring symbol in the play that appears in various scenes specifically when the ghost appears. The ghost explains to the young Hamlet the henbane is poured into the ears of Old Hamlet to kill him. This poison killed him instantly, blocking his blood. Therefore, poisoning a person here in Hamlet symbolizes betrayal, deception, and treachery. This symbol of poison is significant and exposes Claudius evil character.

THE LINGUISTIC SYMBOLISM IN THE TRAGEDY OF OTHELLO, THE MOOR OF VENICE.

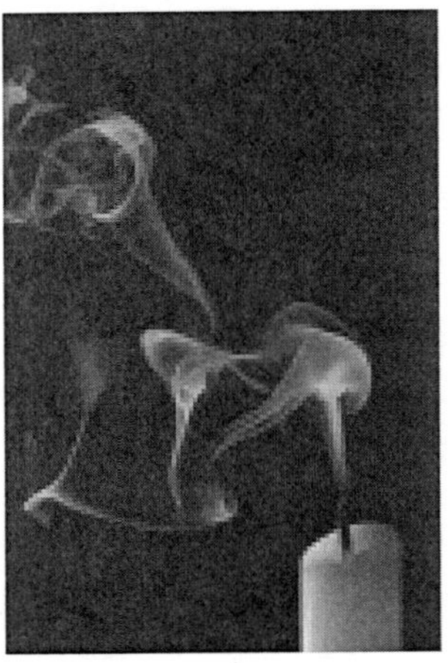

Very important to understand allegories and symbols which Shakespeare uses in *Othello,* since they help to uncover additional layers of meaning in the play and serve as a kind of "imaginary visuals" to the reader, which allow enhancing the emotional burden of the tragedy.

In literature the moon is used very often as allegory of purity, romantic love and chastity. But Shakespeare changes the traditional perception of this image. For instance, his moon alludes to the changeability of fortune and the fickleness of women. The finest example can be found in scene, when Iago convinces Othello that he is being deceived by his wife, after which Othello questions him, referring to Desdemona as the moon: *"Why, why is this?/Think'st thou I'd make a life of jealousy,/To follow still the changes of the moon/With fresh suspicions?/ No. To be once in doubt/Is (once) to be resolved (3.3.210)* Othello believes in Desdemona's purity, yet does not deny her changeable nature, that' s why he is using this allegory, the moon is pure, and nevertheless, it is not constant. Later, when he indicts Desdemona in infidelity he again, relates her to the moon: *"What committed!] Heaven stops the nose at it and the moon winks " (4.2.85).* The moon, once pure, is now seducing. Similarly, Othello believes that Desdemona, once faithful, is betraying him. These two examples are serves as the allegory for the inconstancy of love, and, as a result, the cause of madness: *"It is the very error of the moon. She comes more nearer earth then she was wont /And makes men mad" (5.2.135)* Perhaps, Shakespeare implies that changeability of women, rather then moon was resulted the tragedy.

Another interesting symbol, which Shakespeare uses in his play, is handkerchief, which symbolized Desdemona's honest name, fidelity and her love. With loss of this handkerchief she lost not only Othello's trust, but also her chaste. The pattern is very symbolic, white fabric spotted with red strawberries, that were hand stitched with thread that has been dyed *"in mummy, which the skillful conserved of maidens' hearts" or, virgins' blood (3.4.85).* This handkerchief resembles a wedding sheet with stains of virgin's blood. While Desdemona possessed it, she is honest and faithful. But the moment she lost it, she loses her honest name. Also, within a renaissance period, the handkerchief is a powerful symbol of a woman's romantic favor. Therefore, when Othello sees it in the Cassio's hands, he is convinced that Desdemona is unfaithful and has some feelings for Cassio.

Another interesting symbol is the candle, which symbolizes Desdemona's fragile life. Othello blows out the light just before he strangles Desdemona, and he draws the parallel himself: *"Put out the light, and then put out the light"(5.2.5)* He understands the irreversibility of his actions, as evident from his words: *"If I quench tree, thou flaming minister, /I can again thy former light restore/ Should I repent me. But once put out thy light, /Thou cunning'st pattern of excelling nature,/ I know where is that Promethean heat /That can thy light relume."(5.2.10)* Therefore, this frighteningly poetic parallel, drawn by Shakespeare is another example of "imaginary visuals" that we could find in Othello play.

To conclude, much said about superb language of Shakespeare, his magnificent poetic style, but I particularly like to mention the visual imagery, which he creates with help of his magical linguistic symbolism. It helps the reader to see the entire palette of human emotions through the text, and conceive each mise-en-scene of the play.

Symbolism in "Romeo & Juliet"

Throughout the celebrated play "Romeo and Juliet," William Shakespeare uses symbolism to explore enduring themes such as love, fate and revenge. The play, which tells the tragic story of star-crossed lovers from feuding families, uses a variety of symbols to deepen and reinforce the audience's understanding of the play. Whether referencing the setting or the tragic end of the title characters themselves, these symbols contribute to the feelings of misfortune and despair present in the play.

Light and Darkness

The disparity between lightness and darkness is one of the play's most significant symbols. Innocent, gentile characters like Romeo, Juliet, Mercutio and Benvolio, who display qualities of goodness are often seen during the daylight, while characters who exhibit evil or violence, such as Lord Capulet and Paris, are usually seen only at night. Take Romeo's famous soliloquy, in which he describes Juliet as the giver of light: "But, soft! what light through yonder window breaks? / It is the east, and Juliet is the sun." Contrast that with the speech Prince Escalus gives at the very end of the play, after the death of Romeo and Juliet: "A glooming peace this morning with it brings / The sun, for sorrow, will not show his head."

Poison

Taken in its literal sense, the poison that Romeo acquires from the apothecary is what brings the play to its tragic end. However, the poison symbolizes much more than a toxic potion; rather, it symbolizes the extent of Romeo's love for his beloved Juliet. Upon hearing that she has died, Romeo decides that he cannot live without her, and secures the poison to kill himself at Juliet's tomb: "Here's to my love! O true apothecary! Thy drugs are quick. Thus with a kiss I die." The poison also helps the plot build to its final moment of suspense, in which Juliet awakens and finds Romeo to be dead. Deciding that she cannot live without him, either, she attempts to take the poison from his lips: "O churl! drunk all, and left no friendly drop / To help me after? I will kiss thy lips / Haply some poison yet doth hang on them / To make die with a restorative."

Silver and Gold

Shakespeare uses gold and also silver to explore the pettiness of the feuding between the Capulets and the Montagues. In Act V, when he visits the apothecary, Romeo pays him in gold, stating, "There is thy gold / worse poison to men's souls." This quip highlights Romeo's understanding that above all, money is and has been the impetus for the feuding between the two aristocratic families. As further proof that neither family has learned from the tragedy, both state they will erect golden statues in their deceased children's honor. By contrast, silver represents love and beauty, such as when Romeo states, "How silver-sweet sound lovers' tongues by night" or when a musician claims that "Music has a silver sound."

Blossoms of Tragedy

From Juliet referring to her newfangled relationship as "the bud of love" to her classic line "that which we call a rose by any other name would smell as sweet," plants and flowers, as well as their associated terminology, are used symbolically throughout the play. Shakespeare weaves floral symbolism throughout the play; Romeo, the object of Juliet's affection, is considered a "rose" — a specific flower that symbolizes beauty and love, while Juliet's other suitor — the affable Paris, is considered just a "flower in faith" — pretty, but not special in any way. At the end of the play, after Juliet takes Friar Laurence's sleeping potion to appear dead, her bridal flowers symbolically and paradoxically become her funeral flowers

CHAPTER V

MONOLOGUES

Monologues are devices in theatrical representation that function like asides and soliloquy and apostrophes. A single character, who is delivering the monologue, reveals his most personal thoughts in that given situation. However, unlike soliloquy and dramatic monologues it not supposed to be directed 'at' audience. These thoughts may be introspections and reflections on events that have taken place and also their consequences.

These may also be said to have later evolved to what Virginia Woolf and James Joyce used in their works and came to be called the 'stream-of -consciousnesses. These devices are important in theatre as they are considered to be the unguarded revelation of the character's true nature. It is also often used before the beginning of an action or a plot to also shed light on the events that are unfolding.

The monologues function as revelations of character and analysis of ulterior motives of a character. It sheds light on the motives behind the actions and behaviour of a character. So the vocalization of thoughts in the manner of speech gives access to the inner

workings of the characters mind. It facilitates the formation of the idea of a character and its characterization and helps to assess its motives and also predicting its actions. Monologues are therefore devices in, most notably dramatic literature that help elaborate on the action of the play at the same time not being a part of the action .In later theatrical practices they are somewhere between character portrayal and autobiographical speeches . The monologues in Shakespeare's plays are a most lucid example of how monologues can be used for their effect on the audience . Some examples that stand out are "To be and not to be ..."(*Hamlet* Act III, scene i) and others in Shakespeare's plays . Had it not been for this soliloquy there was no other way to gauge Hamlet's state of excruciating dilemma and the inability to act in the face of obvious treachery . The Prince's cordial and contained behaviour is in stark contrast to his turmoil within and unless the audience is aware of this quiet disquiet in his mind the action in play will lead the audience to think that he is unable to show courage or decisiveness. The fact that his conscientious nature does not allow him to act impulsively would be lost if it was not for the window into in his mind .

To be, or not to be, that is the question:
Whether 'tis nobler in the mind to suffer
The slings and arrows of outrageous fortune,
Or to take arms against a sea of troubles
And by opposing end them. To die—to sleep,
No more; and by a sleep to say we end
The heart-ache and the thousand natural shocks
That flesh is heir to: 'tis a consummation
Devoutly to be wish'd. To die, to sleep;
"To sleep, perchance to dream—ay, there's the rub:
For in that sleep of death what dreams may come,
When we have shuffled off this mortal coil,
Must give us pause—there's the respect
That makes calamity of so long life.
For who would bear the whips and scorns of time,
Th'oppressor's wrong, the proud man's contumely,
The pangs of dispriz'd love, the law's delay,
The insolence of office, and the spurns
That patient merit of th'unworthy takes,
When he himself might his quietus make
With a bare bodkin? Who would fardels bear,
To grunt and sweat under a weary life,

But that the dread of something after death,
The undiscovere'd country, from whose bourn
No traveller returns, puzzles the will,
And makes us rather bear those ills we have
Than fly to others that we know not of?
Thus conscience does make cowards of us all,
And thus the native hue of resolution
Is sicklied o'er with the pale cast of thought,
And enterprises of great pitch and moment
With this regard their currents turn awry
And lose the name of action."

(*Hamlet* Act III, scene i)

It has to be mentioned here that monologue as device originated with the earliest Greek theatre where only a single actor was present on stage with the chorus in the background .The advent of second and third actors evolved later in dramatic convention . It follows that dialogue also evolved later and also after monologue . Hamlet's dilemma of whether to commit suicide is verbalized so that the listener develops an inner perspective of the protagonists mind.

BIBLIOGRAPHY

1. *Ackroyd, Peter (2006). Shakespeare: The Biography. London: Vintage. ISBN 978-0-7493-8655-9.*
2. *Adams, Joseph Quincy (1923). A Life of William Shakespeare. Boston: Houghton Mifflin. OCLC 1935264.*
3. *Baldwin, T.W. (1944). William Shakspere's Small Latine & Lesse Greek.* **1**. *Urbana, Ill: University of Illinois Press. OCLC 359037.*
4. *Barroll, Leeds (1991). Politics, Plague, and Shakespeare's Theater: The Stuart Years. Ithaca: Cornell University Press. ISBN 978-0-8014-2479-3.*
5. *Bate, Jonathan (2008). The Soul of the Age. London: Penguin. ISBN 978-0-670-91482-1.*
6. *"Bard's 'cursed' tomb is revamped". BBC News. 28 May 2008. Retrieved 23 April 2010.*
7. *Bednarz, James P. (2004). "Marlowe and the English literary scene". In Cheney, Patrick Gerard (ed.). The Cambridge Companion to Christopher Marlowe. Cambridge: Cambridge University Press. pp. 90–105. doi:10.1017/CCOL0521820340. ISBN 978-0-511-99905-5 – via Cambridge Core.*
8. *Bentley, G.E. (1961). Shakespeare: A Biographical Handbook. New Haven: Yale University Press. ISBN 978-0-313-25042-2. OCLC 356416.*
9. *Berry, Ralph (2005). Changing Styles in Shakespeare. London: Routledge. ISBN 978-0-415-35316-8.*
10. *Bevington, David (2002). Shakespeare. Oxford: Blackwell. ISBN 978-0-631-22719-9.*
11. *Bloom, Harold (1995). The Western Canon: The Books and School of the Ages. New York: Riverhead Books. ISBN 978-1-57322-514-4.*
12. *Bloom, Harold (1999). Shakespeare: The Invention of the Human. New York: Riverhead Books. ISBN 978-1-57322-751-3.*

13. *Bloom, Harold (2008). Heims, Neil (ed.). King Lear. Bloom's Shakespeare Through the Ages. Bloom's Literary Criticism. ISBN 978-0-7910-9574-4.*
14. *Boas, Frederick S. (1896). Shakspere and His Predecessors. New York: Charles Scribner's Sons. hdl:2027/uc1.32106001899191. OL 20577303M.*
15. *Bowers, Fredson (1955). On Editing Shakespeare and the Elizabethan Dramatists. Philadelphia: University of Pennsylvania Press. OCLC 2993883.*
16. *Boyce, Charles (1996). Dictionary of Shakespeare. Ware, Herts, UK: Wordsworth. ISBN 978-1-85326-372-9.*
17. *Bradbrook, M.C. (2004). "Shakespeare's Recollection of Marlowe". In Edwards, Philip; Ewbank, Inga-Stina; Hunter, G.K. (eds.). Shakespeare's Styles: Essays in Honour of Kenneth Muir. Cambridge: Cambridge University Press. pp. 191–204. ISBN 978-0-521-61694-2.*
18. *Bradley, A.C. (1991). Shakespearean Tragedy: Lectures on Hamlet, Othello, King Lear and Macbeth. London: Penguin. ISBN 978-0-14-053019-3.*
19. *Brooke, Nicholas (2004). "Language and Speaker in Macbeth". In Edwards, Philip; Ewbank, Inga-Stina; Hunter, G.K. (eds.). Shakespeare's Styles: Essays in Honour of Kenneth Muir. Cambridge: Cambridge University Press. pp. 67–78. ISBN 978-0-521-61694-2.*
20. *Bryant, John (1998). "Moby-Dick as Revolution". In Levine, Robert Steven (ed.). The Cambridge Companion to Herman Melville. Cambridge: Cambridge University Press. pp. 65–90. doi:10.1017/CCOL0521554772. ISBN 978-1-139-00037-6 – via Cambridge Core.*
21. *Carlyle, Thomas (1841). On Heroes, Hero-Worship, and The Heroic in History. London: James Fraser. hdl:2027/hvd.hnlmmi. OCLC 17473532. OL 13561584M.*
22. *Casey, Charles (1998). "Was Shakespeare gay? Sonnet 20 and the politics of pedagogy". College Literature. 25 (3): 35–51. JSTOR 25112402.*
23. *Cercignani, Fausto (1981). Shakespeare's Works and Elizabethan Pronunciation. Oxford: Clarendon Press. ISBN 978-0-19-811937-1.*

24. *Chambers, E.K. (1923). The Elizabethan Stage.* **2***. Oxford: Clarendon Press. ISBN 978-0-19-811511-3. OCLC 336379.*
25. *Chambers, E.K. (1930a). William Shakespeare: A Study of Facts and Problems.* **1***. Oxford: Clarendon Press. ISBN 978-0-19-811774-2. OCLC 353406.*
26. *Chambers, E.K. (1930b). William Shakespeare: A Study of Facts and Problems.* **2***. Oxford: Clarendon Press. ISBN 978-0-19-811774-2. OCLC 353406.*
27. *Chambers, E.K. (1944). Shakespearean Gleanings. Oxford: Oxford University Press. ISBN 978-0-8492-0506-4. OCLC 2364570.*
28. *Clemen, Wolfgang (1987). Shakespeare's Soliloquies. London: Routledge. ISBN 978-0-415-35277-2.*
29. *Clemen, Wolfgang (2005a). Shakespeare's Dramatic Art: Collected Essays. New York: Routledge. ISBN 978-0-415-35278-9.*
30. *Clemen, Wolfgang (2005b). Shakespeare's Imagery. London: Routledge. ISBN 978-0-415-35280-2.*
31. *Cooper, Tarnya (2006). Searching for Shakespeare. Yale University Press. ISBN 978-0-300-11611-3.*
32. *Craig, Leon Harold (2003). Of Philosophers and Kings: Political Philosophy in Shakespeare's Macbeth and King Lear. Toronto: University of Toronto Press. ISBN 978-0-8020-8605-1.*
33. *Cressy, David (1975). Education in Tudor and Stuart England. New York: St Martin's Press. ISBN 978-0-7131-5817-5. OCLC 2148260.*
34. *Crystal, David (2001). The Cambridge Encyclopedia of the English Language. Cambridge: Cambridge University Press. ISBN 978-0-521-40179-1.*
35. *de Sélincourt, Basil (1909). William Blake. London: Duckworth & co. hdl:2027/mdp.39015066033914. OL 26411508M.*
36. *Dobson, Michael (1992). The Making of the National Poet: Shakespeare, Adaptation and Authorship, 1660–1769. Oxford: Oxford University Press. ISBN 978-0-19-818323-5.*
37. *Dominik, Mark (1988). Shakespeare–Middleton Collaborations. Beaverton, OR: Alioth Press. ISBN 978-0-945088-01-1.*
38. *Dowden, Edward (1881). Shakspere. New York: D. Appleton & Company. OCLC 8164385. OL 6461529M.*
39. *Drakakis, John (1985). "Introduction". In Drakakis, John (ed.). Alternative Shakespeares. New York: Methuen. pp. 1–25. ISBN 978-0-416-36860-4.*

40. *Dryden, John (1889). Arnold, Thomas (ed.). Dryden: An Essay of Dramatic Poesy. Oxford: Clarendon Press. hdl:2027/umn.31951t00074232s. ISBN 978-81-7156-323-4. OCLC 7847292. OL 23752217M.*
41. *Dutton, Richard; Howard, Jean E. (2003). A Companion to Shakespeare's Works: The Histories. II. Oxford: Blackwell. ISBN 978-0-631-22633-8.*
42. *Edwards, Phillip (1958). Shakespeare's Romances: 1900–1957. Shakespeare Survey.* ***11****. Cambridge: Cambridge University Press. pp. 1–18. doi:10.1017/CCOL0521064244.001. ISBN 978-1-139-05291-7 – via Cambridge Core.*
43. *Eliot, T.S. (1934). Elizabethan Essays. London: Faber & Faber. ISBN 978-0-15-629051-7. OCLC 9738219.*
44. *Evans, G. Blakemore, ed. (1996). The Sonnets. The New Cambridge Shakespeare.* ***26****. Cambridge: Cambridge University Press. ISBN 978-0-521-22225-9.*
45. *Foakes, R.A. (1990). "Playhouses and players". In Braunmuller, A.R.; Hattaway, Michael (eds.). The Cambridge Companion to English Renaissance Drama. Cambridge: Cambridge University Press. pp. 1–52. ISBN 978-0-521-38662-3.*
46. *Fort, J.A. (October 1927). "The Story Contained in the Second Series of Shakespeare's Sonnets". The Review of English Studies. Original Series.* ***III*** *(12): 406–414. doi:10.1093/res/os-III.12.406. eISSN 1471-6968. ISSN 0034-6551 – via Oxford Journals.*
47. *Friedman, Michael D. (2006). "'I'm not a feminist director but…': Recent Feminist Productions of The Taming of the Shrew". In Nelsen, Paul; Schlueter, June (eds.). Acts of Criticism: Performance Matters in Shakespeare and his Contemporaries. New Jersey: Fairleigh Dickinson University Press. pp. 159–174. ISBN 978-0-8386-4059-3.*
48. *Frye, Roland Mushat (2005). The Art of the Dramatist. London; New York: Routledge. ISBN 978-0-415-35289-5.*
49. *Gibbons, Brian (1993). Shakespeare and Multiplicity. Cambridge: Cambridge University Press. doi:10.1017/CBO9780511553103. ISBN 978-0-511-55310-3 – via Cambridge Core.*
50. *Gibson, H.N. (2005). The Shakespeare Claimants: A Critical Survey of the Four Principal Theories Concerning the Authorship of the Shakespearean Plays. London: Routledge. ISBN 978-0-415-35290-1.*

51. *Grady, Hugh (2001a). "Modernity, Modernism and Postmodernism in the Twentieth Century's Shakespeare". In Bristol, Michael; McLuskie, Kathleen (eds.). Shakespeare and Modern Theatre: The Performance of Modernity. New York: Routledge. pp. 20–35. ISBN 978-0-415-21984-6.*
52. *Grady, Hugh (2001b). "Shakespeare criticism, 1600–1900". In de Grazia, Margreta; Wells, Stanley (eds.). The Cambridge Companion to Shakespeare. Cambridge: Cambridge University Press. pp. 265–278. doi:10.1017/CCOL0521650941.017. ISBN 978-1-139-00010-9 – via Cambridge Core.*
53. *Greenblatt, Stephen (2005). Will in the World: How Shakespeare Became Shakespeare. London: Pimlico. ISBN 978-0-7126-0098-9.*
54. *Greenblatt, Stephen; Abrams, Meyer Howard, eds. (2012). Sixteenth/ Early Seventeenth Century. The Norton Anthology of English Literature.* **2**. *W.W. Norton. ISBN 978-0-393-91250-0.*
55. *Greer, Germaine (1986). Shakespeare. Oxford: Oxford University Press. ISBN 978-0-19-287538-9.*
56. *Hales, John W. (26 March 1904). "London Residences of Shakespeare". The Athenaeum. No. 3987. London: John C. Francis. pp. 401–402.*
57. *Holland, Peter, ed. (2000). Cymbeline. London: Penguin. ISBN 978-0-14-071472-2.*
58. *Honan, Park (1998). Shakespeare: A Life. Oxford: Clarendon Press. ISBN 978-0-19-811792-6.*
59. *Honigmann, E.A.J. (1999). Shakespeare: The 'Lost Years' (Revised ed.). Manchester: Manchester University Press. ISBN 978-0-7190-5425-9.*
60. *Jackson, MacDonald P. (2004). Zimmerman, Susan (ed.). "A Lover's Complaint revisited". Shakespeare Studies.* **XXXII**. *ISSN 0582-9399 – via The Free Library.*
61. *Johnson, Samuel (2002) [first published 1755]. Lynch, Jack (ed.). Samuel Johnson's Dictionary: Selections from the 1755 Work that Defined the English Language. Delray Beach, FL: Levenger Press. ISBN 978-1-84354-296-4.*
62. *Jonson, Ben (1996) [first published 1623]. "To the memory of my beloued, The AVTHOR MR. WILLIAM SHAKESPEARE: AND what he hath left vs". In Hinman, Charlton (ed.). The First Folio of Shakespeare (2nd ed.). New York: W.W. Norton & Company. ISBN 978-0-393-03985-6.*

63. *Kastan, David Scott (1999). Shakespeare After Theory. London: Routledge. ISBN 978-0-415-90112-3.*
64. *Kermode, Frank (2004). The Age of Shakespeare. London: Weidenfeld & Nicolson. ISBN 978-0-297-84881-3.*
65. *Kinney, Arthur F., ed. (2012). The Oxford Handbook of Shakespeare. Oxford: Oxford University Press. ISBN 978-0-19-956610-5.*
66. *Knutson, Roslyn (2001). Playing Companies and Commerce in Shakespeare's Time. Cambridge: Cambridge University Press. doi:10.1017/CBO9780511486043. ISBN 978-0-511-48604-3 – via Cambridge Core.*
67. *Lee, Sidney (1900). Shakespeare's Life and Work. London: Smith, Elder & Co. OL 21113614M.*
68. *Levenson, Jill L., ed. (2000). Romeo and Juliet. Oxford: Oxford University Press. ISBN 978-0-19-281496-8.*
69. *Levin, Harry (1986). "Critical Approaches to Shakespeare from 1660 to 1904". In Wells, Stanley (ed.). The Cambridge Companion to Shakespeare Studies. Cambridge: Cambridge University Press. ISBN 978-0-521-31841-9.*
70. *Love, Harold (2002). Attributing Authorship: An Introduction. Cambridge: Cambridge University Press. doi:10.1017/CBO9780511483165. ISBN 978-0-511-48316-5 – via Cambridge Core.*
71. *Maguire, Laurie E. (1996). Shakespearean Suspect Texts: The 'Bad' Quartos and Their Contexts. Cambridge: Cambridge University Press. doi:10.1017/CBO9780511553134. ISBN 978-0-511-55313-4 – via Cambridge Core.*
72. *Mays, Andrea; Swanson, James (20 April 2016). "Shakespeare Died a Nobody, and then Got Famous by Accident". New York Post. Archived from the original on 21 April 2016. Retrieved 31 December 2017.*
73. *McDonald, Russ (2006). Shakespeare's Late Style. Cambridge: Cambridge University Press. doi:10.1017/CBO9780511483783. ISBN 978-0-511-48378-3 – via Cambridge Core.*
74. *McIntyre, Ian (1999). Garrick. Harmondsworth, England: Allen Lane. ISBN 978-0-14-028323-5.*
75. *McMichael, George; Glenn, Edgar M. (1962). Shakespeare and his Rivals: A Casebook on the Authorship Controversy. New York: Odyssey Press. OCLC 2113359.*
76. *Meagher, John C. (2003). Pursuing Shakespeare's Dramaturgy: Some Contexts, Resources, and Strategies in his Playmaking. New*

Jersey: Fairleigh Dickinson University Press. ISBN 978-0-8386-3993-1.

77. *Mowat, Barbara; Werstine, Paul (n.d.). "Sonnet 18". Folger Digital Texts. Folger Shakespeare Library. Retrieved 30 December 2017.*
78. *Muir, Kenneth (2005). Shakespeare's Tragic Sequence. London: Routledge. ISBN 978-0-415-35325-0.*
79. *Nagler, A.M. (1958). Shakespeare's Stage. New Haven, CT: Yale University Press. ISBN 978-0-300-02689-4.*
80. *"Did He or Didn't He? That Is the Question". The New York Times. 22 April 2007. Retrieved 31 December 2017.*
81. *Paraisz, Júlia (2006). The Author, the Editor and the Translator: William Shakespeare, Alexander Chalmers and Sándor Petofi or the Nature of a Romantic Edition. Shakespeare Survey.* **59.** *Cambridge: Cambridge University Press. pp. 124–135. doi:10.1017/CCOL0521868386.010. ISBN 978-1-139-05271-9 – via Cambridge Core.*
82. *Pequigney, Joseph (1985). Such Is My Love: A Study of Shakespeare's Sonnets. Chicago: University of Chicago Press. ISBN 978-0-226-65563-5.*
83. *Pollard, Alfred W. (1909). Shakespeare Quartos and Folios: A Study in the Bibliography of Shakespeare's Plays, 1594–1685. London: Methuen. OCLC 46308204.*
84. *Pritchard, Arnold (1979). Catholic Loyalism in Elizabethan England. Chapel Hill: University of North Carolina Press. ISBN 978-0-8078-1345-4.*
85. *Ribner, Irving (2005). The English History Play in the Age of Shakespeare. London: Routledge. ISBN 978-0-415-35314-4.*
86. *Ringler, William, Jr. (1997). "Shakespeare and His Actors: Some Remarks on King Lear". In Ogden, James; Scouten, Arthur Hawley (eds.). In Lear from Study to Stage: Essays in Criticism. New Jersey: Fairleigh Dickinson University Press. pp. 123–134. ISBN 978-0-8386-3690-9.*
87. *Roe, John, ed. (2006). The Poems: Venus and Adonis, The Rape of Lucrece, The Phoenix and the Turtle, The Passionate Pilgrim, A Lover's Complaint. The New Cambridge Shakespeare (2nd revised ed.). Cambridge: Cambridge University Press. ISBN 978-0-521-85551-8.*
88. *Rowe, Nicholas (1997) [first published 1709]. Gray, Terry A. (ed.). Some Account of the Life &c of Mr. William Shakespear. Retrieved 30 July 2007.*

89. *Rowse, A.L. (1963). William Shakespeare; A Biography. New York: Harper & Row. OL 21462232M.*
90. *Rowse, A.L. (1988). Shakespeare: the Man. Macmillan. ISBN 978-0-333-44354-5.*
91. *Sawyer, Robert (2003). Victorian Appropriations of Shakespeare. New Jersey: Fairleigh Dickinson University Press. ISBN 978-0-8386-3970-2.*
92. *Schanzer, Ernest (1963). The Problem Plays of Shakespeare. London: Routledge and Kegan Paul. ISBN 978-0-415-35305-2. OCLC 2378165.*
93. *Schoch, Richard W. (2002). "Pictorial Shakespeare". In Wells, Stanley; Stanton, Sarah (eds.). The Cambridge Companion to Shakespeare on Stage. Cambridge: Cambridge University Press. pp. 58–75. doi:10.1017/CCOL0521792959.004. ISBN 978-0-511-99957-4 – via Cambridge Core.*
94. *Schoenbaum, S. (1981). William Shakespeare: Records and Images. Oxford: Oxford University Press. ISBN 978-0-19-520234-2.*
95. *Schoenbaum, S. (1987). William Shakespeare: A Compact Documentary Life (Revised ed.). Oxford: Oxford University Press. ISBN 978-0-19-505161-2.*
96. *Schoenbaum, S. (1991). Shakespeare's Lives. Oxford: Oxford University Press. ISBN 978-0-19-818618-2.*
97. *Shapiro, James (2005). 1599: A Year in the Life of William Shakespeare. London: Faber and Faber. ISBN 978-0-571-21480-8.*
98. *Shapiro, James (2010). Contested Will: Who Wrote Shakespeare?. New York: Simon & Schuster. ISBN 978-1-4165-4162-2.*
99. *Smith, Irwin (1964). Shakespeare's Blackfriars Playhouse. New York: New York University Press.*
100. *Snyder, Susan; Curren-Aquino, Deborah, eds. (2007). The Winter's Tale. Cambridge: Cambridge University Press. ISBN 978-0-521-22158-0.*
101. *"Shakespeare Memorial". Southwark Cathedral. Archived from the original on 4 March 2016. Retrieved 2 April 2016.*
102. *Steiner, George (1996). The Death of Tragedy. New Haven: Yale University Press. ISBN 978-0-300-06916-7.*
103. *Taylor, Gary (1987). William Shakespeare: A Textual Companion. Oxford: Oxford University Press. ISBN 978-0-19-812914-1.*
104. *Taylor, Gary (1990). Reinventing Shakespeare: A Cultural History from the Restoration to the Present. London: Hogarth Press. ISBN 978-0-7012-0888-2.*

105. *Wain, John (1975). Samuel Johnson. New York: Viking. ISBN 978-0-670-61671-8.*
106. *Wells, Stanley; Taylor, Gary; Jowett, John; Montgomery, William, eds. (2005). The Oxford Shakespeare: The Complete Works (2nd ed.). Oxford: Oxford University Press. ISBN 978-0-19-926717-0.*
107. *Wells, Stanley (1997). Shakespeare: A Life in Drama. New York: W.W. Norton. ISBN 978-0-393-31562-2.*
108. *Wells, Stanley (2006). Shakespeare & Co. New York: Pantheon. ISBN 978-0-375-42494-6.*
109. *Wells, Stanley; Orlin, Lena Cowen, eds. (2003). Shakespeare: An Oxford Guide. Oxford: Oxford University Press. ISBN 978-0-19-924522-2.*
110. *Gross, John (2003). "Shakespeare's Influence". In Wells, Stanley; Orlin, Lena Cowen (eds.). Shakespeare: An Oxford Guide. Oxford: Oxford University Press. ISBN 978-0-19-924522-2.*
111. *Kathman, David (2003). "The Question of Authorship". In Wells, Stanley; Orlin, Lena Cowen (eds.). Shakespeare: an Oxford Guide. Oxford Guides. Oxford: Oxford University Press. pp. 620–632. ISBN 978-0-19-924522-2.*
112. *Thomson, Peter (2003). "Conventions of Playwriting". In Wells, Stanley; Orlin, Lena Cowen (eds.). Shakespeare: An Oxford Guide. Oxford: Oxford University Press. ISBN 978-0-19-924522-2.*
113. *Werner, Sarah (2001). Shakespeare and Feminist Performance. London: Routledge. ISBN 978-0-415-22729-2.*
114. *"Visiting the Abbey". Westminster Abbey. Archived from the original on 3 April 2016. Retrieved 2 April 2016.*
115. *Wilson, Richard (2004). Secret Shakespeare: Studies in Theatre, Religion and Resistance. Manchester: Manchester University Press. ISBN 978-0-7190-7024-2.*
116. *Wood, Manley, ed. (1806). The Plays of William Shakespeare with Notes of Various Commentators.* **I**. *London: George Kearsley.*
117. *Wood, Michael (2003). Shakespeare. New York: Basic Books. ISBN 978-0-465-09264-2.*
118. *Wright, George T. (2004). "The Play of Phrase and Line". In McDonald, Russ (ed.). Shakespeare: An Anthology of Criticism and Theory, 1945–2000. Oxford: Blackwell. ISBN 978-0-631-23488-3.*
119. *Amir, Âla. "Dramatic Irony In William Shakespeare's Twelfth Night." Journal of Missan Researches 5.9 (2008): 308. Prin*

Creasant